THE
YEAR
I WAS
BORN

Compiler Alison Graham

Signpost Books

Published by Signpost Books, Ltd
25 Eden Drive, Headington, Oxford OX3 OAB

First published 1994
10987654321

Based on an original idea by Sally Wood
Conceived, designed and produced by Signpost Books, Ltd
Copyright on the format Signpost Books, Ltd 1994
Compiler: Alison Graham
Designer: Paul Fry
Editor: Dorothy Wood

ISBN 1 874785 20 1

Acknowledgements: Mirror Group Newspapers plc, for all the pictures in which they hold copyright
and Tom Ashmore for his invaluable help in retrieving them from the files; Hulton Deutsch
Collection, front cover, pp 19, 32, 33; National Motor Museum, Beaulieu, p36.
Every effort had been made to trace all copyright holders, but if any have been inadvertently
overlooked, the publishers will be pleased to make the necessary arrangements
at the first opportunity

Printed and bound in Belgium by Proost Book Production

ME THEN   **ME NOW**

PERSONAL PROFILE

Names:

Date of Birth:

Place of Birth: Time of Birth:

Weight at Birth: Parents' names:

Colour of Eyes: Colour of Hair:

Distinguishing Marks: Weight now:

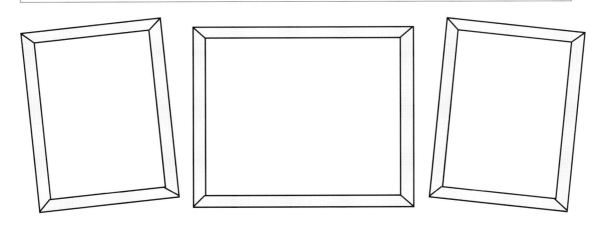

MY FAMILY

1 Monday
New Year's Day

David Lloyd George, *left*, is created an earl in the New Year's honours list. He takes the title Lloyd George of Dwyfor after the mountain stream that runs by his farm.

■ An American newspaper reports that post-war girls will have bigger **curves**. The 32ins bust and 34ins hips will give way to a 38ins bust and 38ins hips.

■ The US Air Force gives a 'sorry we bombed you' **party** for 3,000 schoolchildren in Nantes.

■ The 'Britain at War' exhibition in Brussels is attracting great crowds. Medical students are organising special trips to see the display of up-to-date medical equipment.

2 Tuesday

The first **Nissen** home (kitchen and two other rooms) for bombed-out families in London is unveiled.

■ A 2nd-century roof tile, bearing the foot-marks of a dog chasing a cat made while the tile was laid out to dry, is part of an exhibition of **Roman potter**y found 14ft below Western Union House in Great Winchester Street, London.

■ **Foot and mouth** disease is confirmed in pigs in Paddington. A 15-mile radius is declared an infected area.

3 Wednesday

An 80,000 strong German garrison in Budapest strives to hold out against the Red Army under **Marshal Zhukov,** Stalin's Deputy C-in-C of all the Soviet armies.

■ A 1-mark German Samoa stamp overprinted 'one shilling' by the British in 1914 is sold for £95.

■ **The Duke of Kent** (9) catches the plum pudding thrown from the stage at the London Coliseum during the pantomime Goody Two Shoes.

Afterwards, the royal party go for a ride on the revolving stage.

. . . The national loaf is to be whiter. . .

■ **Kay Summersby**, General Eisenhower's chauffeur, is awarded the BEM in the New Year's honours list. Mrs Summersby has a claim to be the first British woman to enter Paris after the liberation last year.

4 Thursday

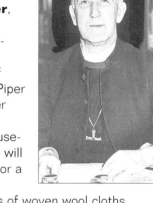

Dr Geoffrey Fisher, *right,* is nominated Archbishop of Canterbury.

■ A new exhibition of **paintings** by John Piper opens at the Leicester Galleries, London.

■ Small stocks of household **rubber gloves** will be available for sale for a few weeks without a permit. Ten new kinds of woven wool cloths are to be added to the utility clothing range.

5 Friday

So sure were the **Japanese** that they were going to occupy Australia that they had their own £1 note printed for circulation there - it measured 6ins x 3ins with a cluster of palm trees on the right hand corner, trailing foliage decorating the edge and bore the words 'The Japanese Government'.

■ **Germany** calls up 12-14-year-olds for compulsory labour.

6 Saturday

Scientists report that there are 50 varieties of **flea** in Britain, but only about 6 are found in houses. They can only jump upwards, and no more than 6ins.

■ All firms in Occupied Holland now allow their employees an extra day off to scrounge in the country for **food** or to buy up potato peelings for 2s. per lb.

■ **Field Marshal Montgomery**, *left,* takes command of all Allied forces north of the German Ardennes Bulge, including the US 1st and 9th Armies. **General**

Omar P Bradley, *right,* commands all troops south of the Bulge.

7 Sunday

Stolen British Army blankets remade into women's coats are the latest **black-market racket** to be discovered by British military police in Brussels.

■ **Canaries** who were taken down to the pit face at Lee Green Collieries yesterday came up none the worse, so 700 miners, idle since a fire last Wednesday, can go back to work.

8 Monday

It is reported from New Delhi that the Hindu ascetic Swami Ram Lakhan Das was **buried alive** in a grave 4 1/2ft deep and 4 1/2ft wide in New Delhi. After being in it for 16 hours he was lifted out apparently lifeless but, after his head had been rubbed with ice and his body massaged, he quickly became normal.

■ Every man on leave from the armed forces can have one bottle of **whisky** at the pre-war price of 21s. if he calls at the Bath Hotel, Glasgow. The stock is provided by whisky magnate **Duncan MacLeod** of Skye. He has lost one son in the war, and has another in a German PoW camp.

9 Tuesday

The **RAF** stages an **exhibition** in one of the biggest department stores in Paris to show the French how the war was fought while Germany cut them off from the rest of the world.

■ A large US force lands at Luzon in the Philippines.

10 Wednesday

The **minimum wage** for agricultural workers is raised by 5s. to £3.10s. per week.

■ Women in Australia have knitted 3,000 woollies for children under five in Fulham, but Dr Edith Summerskill says the mothers must surrender clothing coupons for them.

■ Heating in New York, USA, has been turned down to a maximum 69°F to avert an impending **coal shortage**.

. . . 15ft SNOWDRIFTS in Yorkshire. .

11 Thursday

Berlin Radio reports that only horses engaged in war work are to be allocated a fodder ration. Horses belonging to members of the Nazi party do not come under this new regulation.

■ **King Peter II** of Yugoslavia, who has been living in **exile** in Britain since the Germans invaded his country in 1941, rejects the plan for a regency proposed by **Marshal Tito** and Prime Minister Subasic, as he fears it will devolve power to a single political group without parliamentary control.

. . . Dalwhinnie, Scotland, has 26° of FROST. . .

12 Friday

All **nightclubs** and cabarets in Paris are **closed** to conserve fuel.

■ The Lord Mayor of London receives the first instalment of the 70,000 **toys** sent to him by the Lord Mayor of Melbourne, Cllr Thomas Nettleford, for distribution to the children of London Boroughs. They have been made by housewives, businessmen, wounded soldiers, and even prisoners in Pentridge Gaol, Melbourne.

■ The **snowfall** in the straits of Dover is

the heaviest since 1940.

13 Saturday

Beauty, a six-year-old fox terrier, wins the **Animal VC** for saving the lives of 63 animals from London bomb sites. Her owner says that she goes out on her own, and digs in the debris.
■ The city of **Budapest**, Hungary, is now in the hands of the Russians.

14 Sunday
New moon

Prime Minister Subasic and **Marshal Tito**, *right*, of Yugoslavia, appoint three regents to rule Yugoslavia despite King Peter's reluctance to sign the regency declaration.
■ It is feared that the **IRA** are planning to oversee the escape of 2,000 German PoWs who have just arrived in N. Ireland.
■ The Allied Commission in Italy has printed a million **textbooks** for a re-education campaign to remove fascist doctrines from the minds of Italian children.

15 Monday

The first instalment of a film trilogy on the life of **Ivan the Terrible** is shown to the foreign press in Moscow. It has taken two years to make, and Part II is not yet finished.
■ Col Llewellin, the **Minister of Food**, says that the British **sausage** will soon have 12 1/2% more pork in it, bringing it up to 50%. 'The sausage can now look us in the face,' he says.
■ **General Eisenhower** surprises the staff at an American Army hospital in Paris when he walks in, gives his quota of blood, has a cup of coffee and leaves.

16 Tuesday

The first **civilian boat train** since May 1940 left London yesterday and arrived in Paris today. Up to a few hours before they left, the 200 passengers didn't know what station or port they were leaving from. Most took their own food. More services are expected soon. **Fares**: £5.12s.6d. for 1st class with saloon accommodation; £5.1s.6d. 1st class train/2nd class boat; £3. 8s. 6d. 3rd class boat.
■ **Russian troops** are 55 miles from the German border.

17 Wednesday

Russians liberate **Warsaw**. They are now just 40 miles from the German border.
■ The **Fair Wages** Bill, which gives the Wages Council the power to fix a guaranteed weekly wage and settle holidays, gets an unopposed Second Reading in the House of Commons.
■ British troops in **Burma** cross the Irrawaddy river.

... A new AIRMAIL service between London and Paris carries 700lbs of mail...

18 Thursday

British troops are just a mile from the German border. Eleven capitals have now been liberated: Paris, Brussels, Luxembourg, Athens, Tirana, Belgrade, Rome, Bucharest, Warsaw, Sofia and Helsinki. Six others remain to be freed: Prague, Oslo, Copenhagen, The Hague, Budapest, and Vienna.

■ In Paris, special police are inspecting the cellars of persons suspected of buying **coal** on the **black market**. Where found it is seized and handed to schools and hospitals.

19 Friday

Field Marshal Montgomery's tanks break through the German lines. 'The last battle against Germany is on,' Mr Churchill tells the House of Commons.

■ Anthropologist **Margaret Mead** tells a conference in New York that girls should be taught that spinsterhood isn't a desperate state, and that married life can be overrated.

20 Saturday

President Franklin D Roosevelt, *right,* is inaugurated in Washington, USA. It is his fourth term in office.

■ When the crew of an **RAF Liberator** baled out at night over India, one crew member fell into a tiger trap; another found himself face-to-face with a tiger; a third fell into a tree, and the rest were carried home on elephants which a maharajah had sent out for them.

21 Sunday

Himmler orders every able-bodied man in Silesia to the front line against the Red Army onslaught. Schoolboys, apprentices and office boys join miners called straight from the coal face.

■ **George Formby**, *above,* flies out to entertain the troops in India, Burma and the Far East. He is accompanied by his wife Beryl and has travelled more miles to entertain troops and factory workers than any other British entertainer.

■ Scotland Yard detectives and special Bank of England detectives have been rushed to N. Ireland and Eire to investigate the flood of £5 and £10 notes that have gone into circulation there in the last few weeks.

22 Monday

The **Germans retreat** to the Siegfried Line in the Ardennes.

■ Miss E Strudwick, the headmistress of St Paul's Girls School, London, says that the **BBC** has done a lot of harm to the family life of growing children, and that if the loudspeaker is put on all day, the chance of a child to develop in a normal way is spoiled.

■ A Portsmouth woman is fined £100 and 25gns costs for five offences. She had taken **ration books** as security against loans, and drawn the rations.

■ **Prince Peter of Yugoslavia** dismisses Prime Minister Subasic, who refuses to hand in his resignation, and is preparing to go to Yugoslavia to put the Tito/Subasic agreement into operation.

23 Tuesday

There will be more **colour** in ladies' and children's undies, stockings and ankle socks. There will be two new shades—turquoise and nymph green. London Tan will replace Leap Year in women's stocking colours.
■ The **butter ration** in Eire is reduced from 8 ozs to 6 ozs a week, plus 2 ozs margarine.

24 Wednesday

Admiral Vian leads the biggest British naval force ever sent into action in a purely naval operation. It strikes the Sumatra oil fields which have been producing 75% of Japan's aviation spirit. The refineries are out of action indefinitely.
■ The Red Army is 150 miles from **Berlin**.
. . . The SEA FREEZES along parts of the Straits of Dover. . .

25 Thursday

The government announce that the rebuilding of the **House of Commons** will be completed by 1949 at a cost of £1,250,000.
■ The **Russians** cross the Oder river. The 500,000-strong German army faces encirclement.

26 Friday

King Peter of Yugoslavia dismisses the prime minister Dr Subasic and his government.
. . . ATS recruits want to be sent overseas. . .
■ Marshal Zhukov's **Soviet Army** is now just 100 miles from Berlin.

27 Saturday

The **Duke and Duchess of Gloucester** arrive at Sydney, where the Duke is to take up his appointment as Governor General, but they cannot disembark as a Japanese submarine is prowling near the harbour.
■ **Auschwitz** concentration camp is captured by the Red Army

THE HORRORS

OŚWIĘCIM (AUSCHWITZ) — BIRKENAU.

ОСВЕНЦИМ-БИРКЕНАУ.

AUSCHWITZ-BIRKENAU.

(see panel, above).
■ The **Thames** is **frozen** over from bank to bank 50 yards below Windsor Bridge.

28 Sunday

Full moon

The Soviet Army under **Marshal Gregory Zhukov,** *left,* is little more than 90 miles from Berlin.
■ **ATS** in London become housewives for 10 days in a war office training scheme—they learn how to run a flat, clean, cook, entertain, undertake minor household repairs and go on a shopping expedition. Many of them have never looked after themselves, or a husband, in their lives.
■ The cold weather bites: there are

OF AUSCHWITZ

Although the Allies had known about concentration camps for years, nothing had prepared the shocked soldiers for the horrors they faced as they liberated Auschwitz, Dachau, Belsen, Buchenwald and the rest.

23° of **frost** in the south.

29 Monday

Weather reports from all around the country are seeping out, despite the **censor**. Last week was Scotland's coldest for 50 years, with 10ft snow drifts bringing the railways to a standstill. Whisky **distilleries** are still not working, because the fuel has been diverted to heat shivering householders. A pub at Wigston, Leics, had to close because the beer froze.
■ The Duke and Duchess of Gloucester land in **Australia** at Man of War Steps, in Farm Cove, where Governor Philip landed 157 years ago.

30 Tuesday

The **Duke of Gloucester** is sworn in as

Governor General of Australia. An airliner is to be flown to Australia for the Duke to use on long-distance travel. Three Rolls Royces and a smaller plane belonging to the Duke were in the hold of the ship that took him to Australia.
■ 800 **soldiers** are helping to **distribute coal** in the London area. The very cold weather has disrupted normal transport.

31 Wednesday

Millions of **German refugees** in columns sometimes 30 and 40 miles long, are fleeing before the rapidly advancing Red Army which is 40 miles from Berlin.
■ For the first time in 12 successive nights there was **no frost** last night in the straits of Dover.

FEBRUARY

1 Thursday

An **ambulance** taking Mrs Allen of Gosberton Bank and her hours-old son to hospital in Spalding, Lincs, was dug out of the snow nine times, towed for four miles by a tractor, and finished the journey along a path dug by ARP workers. The 12-mile journey took four hours.

■ The Meat Traders' Association says that almost all British **poultry** is sold on the black market.

■ In a film called *Aerology*, made for the US Army Air Force, **Mickey Mouse** is teaching thousands of war workers how to drive the rivets used in the manufacture of aeroplanes.

■ General Slim's forces are 30 miles west of Mandalay.

2 Friday

Mme Desvignes, one of the founders of a series of French books which have become famous in the **Resistance** movement, is in London. Twenty-five books were written and produced in Paris under the noses of the Gestapo. The number of copies distributed alarmed the Germans so much that they issued 60,000 forged copies containing German propaganda. Mme Desvignes attributes the fact that she evaded capture largely to her reading of many English detective novels.

3 Saturday

The final **battle for Mandalay**, where British and Commonwealth troops, *right*, are involved in heavy fighting, will be filmed by six British newsreel cameramen. The films will be flown back for immediate screening in Britain.

■ **Dr Geoffrey Fisher** is confirmed as Archbishop of Canterbury.

FOOTBALL: A crowd of 66,000 watches England v Scotland at Aston Villa. **England** win 3-2.

4 Sunday

US troops enter **Manila** in the Philippines, just three years and one month after **General MacArthur**, *left*, was forced to quit when the Japanese troops seized it with overwhelming force.

■ A major Allied **raid on Berlin** knocks out most of its eight radio transmitters. Fighter pilots accompanying the bombers see the Russian guns pounding the enemy defences. For the first time the Western **Allies** and the Russians are fighting the same battle in sight of each other.

. . . BELGIUM is clear of German troops.

5 Monday

Winston Churchill and **President Roosevelt** meet in Malta prior to their meeting with Marshal Stalin at Yalta.

■ The Russians on the east bank of the river Oder, facing Berlin, have established numerous **bridgeheads** over the river along a 200-mile front.

■ Staff arriving at the Ministry of Labour and National Service office in Coventry find that **thieves** have got away with 67,400 clothing coupons.

6 Tuesday

A collection of **children's books** dating mainly from the 18th and 19th centuries and including early editions of Oliver Goldsmith's *Little Goody Two Shoes* (first published as *Mrs Margery Two Shoes* in 1766, and a first edition of *Mother Hubbard and Her Dog*, published in 1805), is sold

1945 FACT FILE

World population	2,174 million (1940)
UK population	50,795,000
World's largest city	London (pop. 8,203,942)
Head of State	King George VI (right)
Prime Minster	1) Winston Spencer Churchill (coalition government then caretaker government)
	2) Clement Richard Attlee (from July 27)
House of Commons	Labour have 393 seats, Conservatives 189, Liberals There are 24 women MPs.
UK births	685,544
UK deaths	487,916
UK marriages	343,843
Astronomer Royal	Sir Harold Spencer Jones, W H M Greaves (Scotland)
Poet Laureate	John Edward Masefield, OM
Archbishop of Canterbury	Dr Geoffrey Fisher
Royal Swan Keeper	F T Turk
Licensed motor vehicles	2,938,485 (in 1939 - the last figures available)
Number of telephones	3,600,000
Hottest day	July 15, Norwich 90°F
Coldest day	January 26, Dalwhinnie, -3°F.
Nobel prize winners	Sir Alexander Fleming (Medicine); Gabriele Mistral (Literature) Cordell Hull (Peace)

at Sotheby's for £2,400.

■ A white mice farm from Onderstopoort, South Africa, provided 100,000 white mice for **vaccine** last year.

7 Wednesday

Patrick Clulow of Leicester was sentenced to three months hard labour at Melton Mowbray yesterday on three summonses of **overcharging** for a yard of elastic, a packet of 21 hairpins, and a packet of 58 pins.

■ A very large **Roman pottery** has been found at Bentley, Hants. It contains fragments of all kinds from 5ft jugs to honey pots. Col A G Wade the archaeologist, says it is large enough to have been the Black Country of Roman occupation.

8 Thursday

The Crimea (Yalta) Conference. The Big

Three (USSR, USA and Britain) draw up military plans for the final defeat of Germany.

■ The start of the Canadian First Army offensive at **Nijmegen**, Holland. Allied Army trucks begin to cross the famous bridge.

9 Friday

Herbert Morrison, Home Secretary,

announces that **civilian war casualties** from the out-break of war to September 30, 1944, were: 57,648 missing believed killed, and 79,178 hospitalised. The number of dwellings destroyed were 190,000. Total damaged but repairable is four million.
■ Swiss Radio announce that **Paraguay** has formally declared war on Germany.
■ Two eggs are laid in Croydon Police Court, Surrey, when 19 fowl attend a case in which it is alleged they were stolen.

10 Saturday

New **Allied attack** towards the Rhine. British and Canadian troops gain five miles in first 24 hours. US 7th and French 1st Armies now control about 30 miles of the west bank of the Rhine between Colmar and Mulhouse.
■ Willeys-Overland Motors of Ohio USA have been refused permission to register the word **Jeep** as their trademark. They told the Controller of Trademarks in Dublin that the word was first used to describe a nondescript animal in a *Popeye* cartoon.

11 Sunday

500 homeless **orphaned Dutch children** arrive in Britain. After a meal of Irish stew and milk pudding they board special trains for the Midlands where they are to be put into hostels for a period of quarantine, fitted out with new clothes, given special food to build them up, and taught a little English. When Holland is liberated, it is expected that 20,000 will be given homes in England.
■ **Judy Garland**, *left*, announces her engagement to film director **Vincent Minnelli**.

12 Monday
New moon

The USSR **Marshal Koniev** bursts the Oder line at Ohlau, nr Breslau, opening a possible direct advance to Berlin or Dresden.
■ Government announce that on average 19 people a day are killed by **V-bombs**.
■ British variety artists **Bud Flanagan** and **Chesney Allen**, *above*, say that, for the next 10 years, they will not appear on any programme on the British stage that includes a German, a Japanese or any other former enemy.

13 Tuesday

The **Yalta** Agreement. The Big Three (USA, Britain and the USSR) agree that the Nazi party, the German Army, and all war industry must be destroyed and the Germans must pay reparations in kind for the damage they have done.
■ Marshal Koniev's army races on. It is now 40 miles beyond the Oder. On the western front, Montgomery's men are through the second belt of the **Siegfried Line**.

14 Wednesday
Ash Wednesday, St Valentine's Day

Many Coventry mothers who lost children in the Blitz have asked to adopt the Dutch **orphans** who are staying nearby.
■ Bradford has adopted the urban district of Coulsdon and Purley under the good neighbour scheme. Three van loads of goods—furniture and kitchen utensils—have been sent. Two more loads are on the way.

15 Thursday

A gift of 37 **dolls** from Ms Margaret Gleason, an invalid of Berkeley, California, has been distributed to children injured in air raids in Britain by the Ministry of Health at her request.

■ CSM **Denis Compton**, former Arsenal footballer, *left,* has taken up cricket exclusively and may never appear in big-time football again.

16 Friday

Marshal Koniev's army is only 50 miles from Dresden.
■ **Family Allowances** Bill proposes that the allowance should be paid to the father. The mother can only have the money paid to her provided she can prove to the magistrate that her husband drinks with the money, gambles it away, or otherwise withholds it. The Women Six Point Group, who work for sex equality, have asked **Edith Summerskill** to raise the matter in the Commons.
■ The **Venezuelan** Government announces that it recognises the existence of a state of war with Germany and Japan.

17 Saturday

Vilma Suberley Jones of Jones Prairie, Texas, has confessed to **marrying** at least **eight men** in the last five years, and getting £1,150 in allotment cheques. Vilma has been blonde, titian, and brunette, and has used 28 names. She handled her husbands so well that none of them knew he wasn't the only man in her life.

■ Lady Denman, director of the Women's Land Army, resigns in protest at the government's refusal to confer the same special post-war benefits on the WLAs as members of the forces.

18 Sunday

Someone with ambitions to **paint** the town red started with the statue of Progress on the Victoria Memorial in front of Buckingham Palace. The statue will be cleaned tomorrow.

Peter Brough and **Archie Andrews**, *above,* return to radio tomorrow on 'Monday Night at Eight'. Many people who write to Archie Andrews mention his partner Brough, not seeming to realize that Archie is a ventriloquist's dummy. Once on tour, Peter Brough found that the theatre manager had given them separate dressing rooms!
■ It is the **warmest February** day in London for 40 years: 62°F at 5pm.

19 Monday

There are reports from Los Angeles of a **gearless car** that runs without petrol but uses compressed air and vapour from a mysterious green fluid. It is greeted with

FEBRUARY

BOOKS OF THE YEAR

ANIMAL FARM	George Orwell (far right)
WILLIAM THE SILENT	C.V. Wedgewood
(winner of the James Tait Black Memorial Award)	
A BELL FOR ADANO	John Hersey
(winner of the Pulitzer Prize)	
BRIDESHEAD REVISITED	Evelyn Waugh (right)
JOSEPH THE PROVIDER	Thomas Mann
FOREVER AMBER	Kathleen Winsor
THE COMMODORE	C.S. Forester
ISLAND IN THE SKY	E.K. Gann
THUNDERHEAD	Mary O'Hara
THE BUILDING OF JALNA	Mazo de la Roche
LONDON BELONGS TO ME	Norman Collins
DIED IN THE WOOL	Ngaio Marsh

scepticism by the US and UK motor industries.

■ Since the outbreak of war, more than 8,000 **Scottish girls** have chosen husbands from among troops of other countries.

■ US Marines land on **Iwo Jima**, *below*, 750 miles from Tokyo.

20 Tuesday

Children's boots and shoes will have better and more hard-wearing soles, says the President of the National Boot and Shoe Manufacturers Federation.

■ **Mr Churchill** and **President Roosevelt** meet in **Cairo** to discuss the war in Japan.

21 Wednesday

The Ministry of Agriculture says the government is giving sympathetic consideration to the problem of treating the 65,000 women of the **Land Army** on the same basis for war gratuity purposes as women in the services.

■ Marshal Zhukov's army is **34 miles from Berlin**.

22 Thursday

Preparations are being made in London to arrange homes for 7,000 homeless Dutch children.

■ **Greece** declares itself in favour of becoming a Republic.

23 Friday

6,000 Allied **bombers** in raid on German rail, road and canal systems.

FOOTBALL: Nearly 10,000 queue in Glasgow for tickets for the England v Scotland match to be played at Hampden Park on April 14. The first of the fans took their places on the street as early as 8pm on Wednesday night.

■ **Turkey** and **Uruguay** declare war on Germany.

24 Saturday

Cambridge win the **Boat Race** by two lengths—in a boat they borrowed from Oxford.

■ Between now and the end of March the last 200 of over 1,000 British and American heavy locomotives will be withdrawn from service with British railways and sent overseas to the fighting fronts in Europe.

. . . ALEXEI TOLSTOI (62), famous Russian novelist and dramatist, dies. . .

FOOD FLASH: 5-6 boatloads of dessert `apples` have arrived from Canada and the USA; bitter **oranges** are expected soon; sweet oranges will follow; 33,600 **rabbits** have arrived in London from Ireland.

25 Sunday

The Park Hotel, Lockport, NY, has only Butch, a black-and-white fox **terrier,** as **pageboy.** For two years Butch has never failed to deliver post, newspapers and keys to residents. Grateful patrons tip the dog with biscuits, sweets and even steak.
■ German sources admit that Marshal Zhukov is within 35 miles of **Danzig.**

USELESS EUSTACE

"Tck! Tck! My memory. What did we say we were doing tomorrow?"

26 Monday

Foundation Day, Australia

Bilious **canaries** save soldiers' lives. Experimenters at ICI discovered that when canaries are exposed to certain gases, they throw up their food. In the digested food is mepacrine, which is a substitute for quinine. The Japanese took all our sources of supply of quinine in the Far East. Mepacrine is now in general use in hospitals, and so effective is the drug that a man suffering from **malaria** is fit in a week.

27 Tuesday

Full moon

Allied troops are just 13 miles from **Cologne.**
■ Nine **girls** have been decorated as **Heroines of the Soviet Union.** Among them are Natalia Metlin (22), who has been on 840 bombing raids, and Guards Captain Olga Shansirova, leader of a squadron, who was killed while flying over Germany.

FOOD FACTS —1

Take advantage of the fine HERRING HARVEST

HERRINGS are a remarkable fish: they give you more nourishment for your money than a cut of the joint; eg. they give you warmth and energy, and they give you two important extras—the protective vitamins A and D. Herrings are at their best just now. So let's make the most of them while they are here.

TO CLEAN HERRINGS: Hold the fish firmly round the middle. With kitchen scissors cut almost through the fish from the back just below the head. Take the head in your hand and give it a twist and a pull. This pulls out the unwanted insides as well. Cut off the tail. Scrape the fish well from tail towards head with a blunt knife to take off scales. Wash thoroughly.

Easy ways to cook Herrings

GRILLED HERRINGS. Grease the grill grid with a very little fat. Lay the fish on the hot grill. Cook briskly for a few minutes on each side until herrings are crisp and brown. Serve with mustard sauce or a sharp sauce.

BAKED STUFFED HERRINGS
(for 4 people)
1 large or 2 small herrings per person
FOR THE STUFFING: 2 oz breadcrumbs, a small onion, grated or chopped, 1/2 level teaspoonful of mixed herbs; 1 level tablespoonful dried egg (reconstituted), or a little milk, salt and pepper to taste, 3 level tablespoons chopped parsley.

Bone the fish. Mix the ingredients for the stuffing, binding with the milk or reconstituted egg. Spread stuffing on the underside of each herring. Roll up from the tail end, pack into a greased pie-dish, sprinkle fish with salt and pepper. Cover with greased paper. Bake in a moderate oven for 20mins. Sprinkle with chopped parsley and serve in the dish in which they were cooked.

THE MINISTRY OF FOOD, LONDON, W.1.

28 Wednesday

Boots the Chemist are giving all their employees an extra week's summer holiday to counteract war strain.

■ The German battle line west of the Rhine is broken.

■ Churchill offers citizenship to **Poles** who don't want to go home. It is believed that the offer will be extended to all who have helped us and can produce a good reason for not going home.

. . . It is announced that the COAL RATION for March will be 5cwt per household. . .

MARCH

1 Thursday
St David's Day

British Gloster **Meteor** jets, the first jet planes, are in action over Germany

■ President Roosevelt has presented **King Ibn Saud** of Saudi Arabia with a wheelchair. The king was so fascinated when he saw the President's that Mr Roosevelt took the hint and found a spare one, which he gave to the king.

■ The **Queen, Princess Elizabeth** and **Princess Margaret** are among those who knitted sweaters, scarves and gloves for the men of the Royal Navy in the last five years

2 Friday

Four **nurses** are **fined** for passing love letters to German PoWs. The policeman investigating said that at first he had thought the nurses might be assisting the prisoners to escape, but by the time his enquiries had ceased, he was satisfied it was only a serious case of fraternization.

■ Children's wellington boots are to be imported from Canada in limited numbers—maximum retail price 11s.8d.—13s.8 1/2d. They will go to retailers in small market towns to be sold for the use of country children, who need them most.

DOING HER BIT: Princess Elizabeth learns valuable map-reading and mechanic's skills, and shows off the latter under the gaze of her mother, the Queen

3 Saturday

Ex-Hollywood star, **Madeleine Carroll**, now a Red Cross nurse in France, says she has finished with film work forever. She is giving up her career to look after 200 French war orphans who are living at her home, Saudreville, outside Paris.

■ **King Peter** of Yugoslavia has selected the three regents who will represent him in Yugoslavia.

■ Cambridge wins the **Varsity rugby** match by two goals and two tries to a dropped goal.

4 Sunday

Princess Elizabeth (18) joins the **ATS**. Her rank is second subaltern, and she is immediately sent on a truck-driving course. A Home Office adviser recommends that

PRINCESS ELIZABETH JOINS THE ATS

schools should keep canvas bags at the ready to lower small children out of the window in case of fire.
■ Gangster **Al Capone**'s younger brother, Matt—the only 'good' one of Mrs Capone's five children —is charged with the murder of a racetrack tout, who was killed and thrown from a car in Chicago.

5 Monday

Invitations are sent to 45 nations to attend a conference in San Francisco to prepare the **United Nations Charter.**
■ A 'honeymoon hostel' has just been opened in Brussels by the YWCA for newly married service men and women. The building was used by German troops during the occupation.
■ **Women's earnings** have doubled since October 1938. The average weekly wage is now 64s.3d. (Men's average weekly wage is 124s.4d.)

6 Tuesday

Strike at London Docks. 3,000 troops handle cargoes.
■ **Sweden** launches the 'Yellow Duck' campaign to collect toys for children in liberated Europe.
■ The first cloistered **nun** to go on the air broadcasts from the 300 year-old Ursuline Monastery in Quebec, in support of the Canadian Red Cross campaign.
■ **Marshal Tito** is confirmed as undisputed leader of Yugoslavia.

7 Wednesday

Field Marshal **Montgomery's mother** says that she has made a bet that the war will be over by March 23 next. She has written to her son and told him to see that she doesn't lose her bet!
■ Sabu, the **elephant boy** of the films, *right,* has been awarded the US DFC. He was the tail gunner in a Liberator bomber, flying through anti-aircraft fire to sink Japanese ships off Borneo.

■ The US 1st Army crosses the **bridge at Remagen**, 12 miles south of Bonn, the first bridgehead across the Rhine.

8 Thursday

Archie Andrews, the ventriloquist's dummy, receives his first income tax assessment form.
■ Film star **Red Skelton**, *left,* announces that he is going to marry Georgia Maureen Davies this week—and have his tonsils attended to as well.

9 Friday

The US 1st and 3rd Armies join up at Remagen. **Bonn** is now in US hands.

■ The second reading of the **Family Allowances** Bill. There will be a free vote in committee on whether allowances should be paid to the mother or the father. There is almost unanimous support for paying the weekly allowance of 5s., which will come into force after the war, direct to the mother.

10 Saturday

Mrs Edwards of Noss Mayo, Devon, rested her basket by a wall to watch the hunt assemble. When she picked it up she had lost five **meat rations** and 1lb of sausages, all eaten by the hounds.

■ Folkestone's **clocks,** some of which are visible from the sea, are being blacked out again.

11 Sunday

Another 600 Dutch **orphans arrive** in Britain. Holland itself is stricken by a **famine** the like of which has not been seen outside the Balkans or the Far East for centuries. The country is without gas, electricity, transport or fuel, and all medical equipment, medicines and operating equipment have been removed from Amsterdam's main hospital.

12 Monday

Anne Frank, *left*, author of the famous diary, dies in the Bergen-Belsen concentration camp.

■ It is announced that a new **air mail** service goes into operation between Britain and Australia next month. It will ensure that mail reaches Britain in less than a week.

13 Tuesday

Demobilization plans announced. The House of **Commons** reverts to afternoon and evening sittings.

■ 4,300 tons of **seed potatoes** are sent to Italy to be distributed to farmers in the principal potato growing areas, after the failure of their own seed potato crop.

14 Wednesday

New moon

Because 'nobody looks at a woman's legs before lunchtime', the president of the American National Association of Hosiery Manufacturers is asking women to go without **stockings** in the mornings, as rayon is in short supply.

■ **Heinz & Co** demonstrate tins of self-heating food, which produce hot food in three minutes.

15 Thursday

The **Duke of Windsor**, *left*, resigns his governorship of the Bahamas.

. . . Nineteen government FACTO-RIES revert to peacetime production. . .

■ In a desperate attempt to get supplies through to the front the Germans are trying new forms of **camouflage**. RAF pilots have spotted a line of stationary trains

with a full set of tracks, complete with sleepers and bolts, painted on the top of the train.

16 Friday

One of four escaped **German PoWs** captured at Castle Bromwich, Warks, 110 miles from their camp at Bridgend, S Wales, said they had passed hundreds of people, but nobody seemed to take much notice. All four wore German mackintoshes, and one still wore his German forage cap. Three more prisoners are still at liberty.

■ **Iwo Jima** in the Philippines is now in US hands, Joe Rosenthal's Pulitzer Prize-winning picture, right. In Europe, the US 1st Army cuts the Ruhr-Frankfurt road.

17 Saturday
St Patrick's Day

Bing Crosby, and **Ingrid Bergman**, *below right*, win Oscars for Best Actor and Best Actress in *Going My Way* and *Gaslight*. Barry Fitzgerald is best supporting actor in *Going My Way*, and Ethel Barrymore best supporting actress in *None But the Lonely Heart*. The Best Production award went to *Going My Way*.

■ Non-priority **milk** allowance for adults is increased from 2 to 2 1/2 pints per week.

18 Sunday

Hitler has instituted a new medal—a badge to be given to those who shoot down low-flying planes with hand weapons or small-bore automatic arms.

■ Twelve black-footed Cape **penguins** are due to arrive by plane for London Zoo any moment now.

■ All schools and universities in Japan are closed, and everyone over the age of **six** is ordered to do war work.

19 Monday

The funeral of **Lord Alfred Douglas** (74),

whose life had been haunted by the Oscar Wilde scandal. Among those attending are the Marquess of Queensberry, Lord Tredegar, and the actor Donald Sinden.

■ A Birmingham scientist has developed a blue-tinged **window** glass that keeps people cool, but turns the heat on flies—it's just too hot for them to walk on.

■ The last three German PoWs who **tunnelled** their way out of Bridgend last week are back in custody.

20 Tuesday

News that there may be a further reduction in the **meat ration** in Britain spurs the Victoria Chamber of Agriculture in Australia to suggest a reduction of 20% in their own

ration to allow further supplies to be sent to the UK. The government proposes reducing the ration by 5%, which would supply only 25,000 tons out of the 150,000 tons needed to supply the meagre UK ration.

21 Wednesday

The Government confirm that the **National Health Service** scheme will be open to everyone.
■ The Ministry of Food show how the British meat ration is made up: USA, 2d., Domestic, 5d., S America, 4 1/2d., Australia and New Zealand 2d., Canada 1/2d.

22 Thursday

Soviet troops break through in **Silesia**. 15,000 German troops surrender. General **von Rundstedt** is sacked, and **Kesselring** is appointed Commander-in-Chief in the West.
■ **Queen Wilhelmina** of the Netherlands, *left,* on a 10-day trip home, the first time she has been there for four years, tours the flooded areas seated in an armchair on a 'duck'. Thousands scramble to see her, and she talks to people still living in the upper rooms of their houses, with sea water lapping half-way up their front doors.

23 Friday

Field Marshal **Montgomery**'s 21st Army Group **cross the Rhine** nr. Wesel.
■ Cricketer **Len Hutton** is to play as an amateur for Pudsey St Lawrence in the Bradford League. He will also appear in a few charity matches.

24 Saturday

Brighton beach will reopen today. All mines have been cleared, *right.*
■ The first French Line ship since 1940 has docked in New York with a **luxury** cargo of cognac and French perfume.

25 Sunday

Vice-President **Truman** opens the San Francisco Conference to frame the constitution of the United Nations.

■ One of the last V1-**flying bombs** to descend on London lands near Marble Arch, blowing out the windows of the Hyde Park Hotel suite occupied by author **Evelyn Waugh**. Pictured above is one that didn't hit its target.
■ Winston Churchill accompanies Field Marshal Montgomery on a visit to the troops across the Rhine *(Picture, facing page).*

26 Monday

Former prime minister and World War I leader, **David Lloyd George** (72), dies peacefully in his sleep at his home in Wales.
■ Easter holidaymakers on the north east coast are officially warned to beware of minefields.
■ The MP for Salisbury disobeyed government orders to cultivate food on his land on the Isle of Islay in the Western Highlands, and is fined £30.

27 Tuesday

Women and girls in the south of England are losing their hair through shock, or it is becoming prematurely grey. Leading **wig-makers** are booked up until the

end of the year. Genuine victims of V-bombs will receive priority treatment.

■ The US Department of Agriculture has developed an onion-peeling machine. A jet of steam blasts off the outer skin.

■ The last **doodlebug** falls on England.

■ US troops enter **Frankfurt.** General collapse of German forces on the Western Front.

28 Wednesday
Full moon

The Ministry of Food advises those going away for **Easter** to take food and soap with them.

■ The Technical Advisory Committee urges the rebuilding of the **coal** industry on the most modern lines with area amalgamations and a central authority with statutory powers.

■ Funeral of **Steve Donoghue** (60), the famous jockey who rode six Derby winners. He died on March 23.

29 Thursday

Comedian **Vic Oliver** is granted a divorce on the grounds of desertion by his wife, the **prime minister's daughter**, WAAF Section Officer Sarah Churchill, *left*.

■ Holidaymakers are warned to look out for mines even on safe beaches.

30 Friday
Good Friday

Funeral of **David Lloyd George**. He is buried on a hillside overlooking his home.

■ Flt Lt Graham of Glasgow left Newfoundland in a Canadian-built **Mosquito** of RAF transport command after breakfast this morning, and arrived in

Scotland in time for a late lunch, making a record-breaking west-east crossing of 5hrs 38mins. The previous record was set in 1943 by a fully laden Liberator that took 6hrs 12mins.

31 Saturday

Danzig taken by the Russians.

■ A British government mission discusses food problems in Washington. Mrs Roosevelt says that if the Americans could eat British **rations** for one month they would be more satisfied with what they have.

APRIL

1 Sunday
Easter Sunday

The **cheese** ration is cut from 3oz to 2oz per week. Caterers may now use milk—liquid, powdered or condensed—to make ice cream.

■ Soviet troops are just 33 miles from **Vienna.**

2 Monday

Field Marshal Montgomery's 21st Army Group is 100 miles over the Rhine.

■ Launchings of VI and V2 flying bombs are much reduced as Canadian troops enter the launch sites in NW Holland.

■ South and East coast resorts report a gloomy **Easter.** Any crowds went home early as near-gale-force winds and heavy seas made their presence felt.

APRIL

3 Tuesday

In its first public **weather forecast** since September 2, 1939, the Air Ministry announce that frost is expected in SE Scotland, England and Wales, excluding western central districts.

■ The British Government signs an agreement with **Canada** for all the beef, bacon, ham and eggs that Canada can supply until the end of 1946.

■ Between 50,000-100,000 German troops are in the Ruhr, surrounded by the **steel ring** of Montgomery's and Bradley's troops. In March on the Western Front, the Allies took 350,000 prisoners.

4 Wednesday

300 square miles of the **Netherlands** has now been liberated.

■ The Ministry of Home Security begins to wonder what it will do with 45 million **gas masks** and home shelters.

5 Thursday

Conductor **Leopold Stokowski** (63), once **Greta Garbo**'s great love, is to marry mil-

Princess Elizabeth at the Cup Final.

lionairess Gloria Vanderbilt (21).

■ **Coal** is so short that practically every train but the **Flying Scotsman** has to run on briquettes (coal dust formed into lumps), and that, say the railways, is why some trains run up to half a day late.

■ The **yachting** waters of the Solent are open again for sailing, fishing and pleasure boating, as are Southsea, Ryde, Bembridge, Shanklin, Sandown, Ventnor and Freshwater Bay.

6 Friday

Russia ends its Peace Pact with Japan.

■ Black marketeers are trying to corner seats for the anticipated **victory parade** in London. Some shopkeepers on the route will make enough money to pay their year's rent.

■ **Planning** experts say that Britain will need 50 new garden cities after the war.

German REFUGEES flee Bremen, Hamburg and Hanover.

7 Saturday

The King and Queen, with Princess Elizabeth, *above*, King Haakon and Prince Olaf of Norway, General Lord Wavell, and Allied ministers and military leaders plus 90,000 spectators who pay £29,000 for the privilege, watch the **FA Cup Final** at Wembley. Chelsea beat Milwall 2-0.

■ Actor **James Cagney** buys a novel, *The Lion in the Streets*, from author, Adria Locke Langley, a champion woman riveter at a Los Angeles aircraft plant, for $25,000.

■ American troops are just 110 miles from **Berlin**.

8 Sunday

Germany's **gold** reserves, 100 tons of gold

and millions in currency, are **found in saltmines** near Gotha, together with art treasures from the national art galleries including pictures by Raphael, Rembrandt, van Dyke and Dürer. There are also 120 cases of Goethe's manuscripts. The total worth is estimated at hundreds of millions of pounds.

9 Monday

Duty-free canned **beer** at 2d. per pint may be sent to serving men overseas after being paid for by relatives in the UK.
■ Thousands of children go to primary **school** for the first time. Elementary schools have ceased to exist. Secondary schools, which take children above the age of 11, will open soon.

10 Tuesday

Shirley Temple (nearly 17) is to marry Sergeant John Agar (24), left. Mrs Temple said the wedding would not be for two or three years yet.
■ Women's feet are getting bigger. Sizes 5 and 5 1/2 used to be the most popular sizes, now it's 6 and 6 1/2.
■ **General Eisenhower** is getting as much fan mail as Frank Sinatra.

11 Wednesday

US troops capture Hanover. Field Marshal Montgomery's 21st Army Group races for **Hamburg**.
■ Parents place this **advertisement** in a Surrey newspaper:

A young lady of 6, shortly returning from the USA to live in Weybridge, who probably knows all the answers, needs an English governess who is willing to learn.

12 Thursday

New moon

The **Swedes,** who have been neutral throughout the war, are trying to arrange for

King Leopold of the Belgians, *left*, now a PoW, to be released by the Germans. It is said that King Leopold intends to abdicate and live in Sweden.
■ The Government announce that there will be no official State VE-Day **celebrations,** as so many troops are still serving in other war theatres.
■ Hurstmonceux Castle, Sussex, is to be the new home of the **Royal Observatory**.

13 Friday

President Roosevelt (63), **dies** at his home in Warm Springs, Georgia. At 1 o'clock he was sitting for preliminary sketches for a portrait. He lost consciousness very quickly, and died at 3.34pm. Vice-President **Harry S. Truman**, *right,* a one-time Kansas City haberdasher, **becomes president**. The King orders one week's Court mourning.
■ The first of 20,000 Phoenix **temporary homes** is handed over to Salsburgh, nr. Glasgow. It is a single storey, and took only six days to build.

14 Saturday

There will be no official rationing of potatoes this season.
■ The first **salad** special, or 'Penzance Perishable', arrived in London carrying 50,000 lettuces, 22 tons of onions, cucumbers, radishes, cabbage and watercress. But salad won't be cheap. Lettuces will cost up to 1s., watercress 2s. a bundle, radishes about 8d., cucumbers 10d., and onions and cabbage will be 10d. and 4 1/2d. per lb.
■ The government have agreed to the **ATS** serving **overseas**, on the following condi-

■ The **Wellington** bomber goes out of service. . .

tions: No ATS girl with family ties will serve overseas; no married women, or those under 21 or over 40; those on AA operational duties; an only child of one remaining parent; those posted at home on compassionate grounds, and those who enlisted for home service only. Also, the fiancé of a girl who is himself overseas, may apply for her to be retained at home if he is returning in 12 months and intends to marry her on his return.

15 Sunday

President **Roosevelt** is **buried** in the garden of his family home, Hyde Park, in the Hudson Valley, New York State, at 4 p.m. BDST (British Daylight Saving Time). Anthony Eden, Lord Halifax, and the Earl of Athlone attend on behalf of the British government.
■ Today is the 199th anniversary of the battle of **Culloden**.

16 Monday

Twenty-two indignant **girl footballers** in Bristol defend their right to play the game. Comments from outside range from 'Disgraceful'—a mother, to 'Undignified'—the Rector of Weymouth, and, 'If they had been playing up North no one would say a word. Lassies have been playing football for years.'
■ The coaches and horses of the Royal Mews get in some practise for the **Victory** drive.

17 Tuesday

Another 7,000 **British PoWs** are freed, but no names will be listed until the next of kin have been informed.
■ **General Slim** thanks his men (one of them, pictured right) for their magnificent victory in Central Burma.
■ A memorial service for President Roosevelt is held at St Paul's Cathedral.

18 Wednesday

The **Labour** party's **manifesto** for the forthcoming election includes plans to nationalise the Bank of England, and the public ownership of fuel, power, inland transport, and the iron and steel industries.
■ Dr **Thomas Wood**, the musician, has returned from a 70,000-mile tour of Australia, India and Burma, with a 3ft long, vividly coloured grass skirt for the Queen made by the women of Papua, New Guinea.

19 Thursday

Leipzig falls. The Russians are 20 miles from Berlin.
■ **Italian PoWs** will be employed as dustmen by Ashby-de-la-Zouche council. They will be paid 1s.9d. per hour.
■ Wing Commander 'Tin Pin' **Douglas Bader**, right, is released from PoW camp in Germany.
■ In answer to public outcry, the Secretary for Air says that it would not be in the public interest to reintroduce full **weather** reports for farmers.
. . . Geoffrey Fisher is enthroned as ARCHBISHOP of Canterbury. . .

20 Friday

All **blackout** restrictions will be lifted next Monday, April 23, except in a five-mile belt around the coast. Mr Morrison, the Home Secretary, asks that should there be an alert, people draw their blinds and put out the lights. Drapers anticipate a rush to buy curtains.
■ **Adolf Hitler** celebrates his 56th birthday.

WHAT'S ON AT THE THEATRE

The Royal Family, *pictured right*, enjoying the Royal Variety Performance. **Lupino Lane**, *left,* scored a hit in *Me and My Girl*.

There were a host of fine shows and strong performances on the London stage, providing a distraction from the toils of war.

THE HASTY HEART	Frank Leighton and Margaretta Scott
PRIVATE LIVES	John Clements, Kay Hammond, Raymond Huntley, Peggy Simpson
THE NIGHT AND THE MUSIC	Vic Oliver
SEE HOW THEY RUN	Ronald Simpson and Joan Hickson
THE RIVALS	Anthony Quayle and Edith Evans
A MIDSUMMER NIGHT''S DREAM	John Gielgud and Peggy Ashcroft
PERCHANCE TO DREAM	Ivor Novello
DUET FOR TWO HANDS	John Mills, Mary Morris and Elspeth March
UNCLE VANYA	Laurence Olivier and Ralph Richardson
THE FIRST GENTLEMAN	Robert Morley
THE SKIN OF OUR TEETH	Cecil Parkinson and Vivien Leigh
JAKOBOWSKY AND THE COLONEL	Michael Redgrave and Rachel Kempson
SIGH NO MORE	Joyce Grenfell
FINE FEATHERS	Jack Buchanan
ME AND MY GIRL	Lupino Lane and Valerie Tandy

FROM left: Joyce Grenfell, Robert Morley, Edith Evans, Peggy Ashcroft, John Clements and Ralph Richardson

FOOD FACTS —2

Potatoes are precious

When potatoes are scarce, they are more precious than ever. Here are some suggestions for avoiding waste in preparation and for some filling dishes to serve with or instead of potatoes.

Potato-saving Tips

1. Remember that as much as 25% is wasted by peeling potatoes. If peeling is necessary, peel very thinly.
2. 'A potato fast boiled is a potato spoiled'. To stop potatoes breaking up and going to waste, boil steadily but don't gallop.
3. To prevent potatoes going black, add a little vinegar to the water.

To 'help out' with the potatoes

Serve these dishes with meat, fish, etc., as fillers and to supply energy. But remember, because they lack vitamin C —the vitamin potatoes contain—always serve with them another vitamin-rich vegetable—cabbage, savoy, Brussels sprouts, cauliflower, kale, parsley, watercress, swedes or bottled tomatoes, whichever is available.

PLAIN DUMPLINGS WITHOUT FAT

Ingredients: 4 oz flour, 2 level teaspoons of baking powder, 1 dried egg, DRY*, I level teaspoon salt, water to mix. *Quantity:* for 4 people. *Method:* Mix together the flour, baking powder, dried egg and salt. Add enough water to mix to a soft dough. Cut the mixture into 12 portions. Shape roughly into dumplings with the hands. Drop into boiling soup or water, and cook for 10 minutes. Drain and serve instead of potatoes.

POPOVERS

Ingredients: 4 oz flour, 1 dried egg, DRY*, 1/2 pint milk and water, 2 tablespoons water, 1 knob dripping or fat. *Quantity:* for 4 people. *Method:* Mix egg, flour and salt with sufficient milk to make a stiff mixture. Beat well, add the rest of the milk and water. Heat the fat until smoking hot in small cake tins, or large patty pans, then pour the batter into the tins. Cook in a brisk oven for about 20 minutes.

* One level tablespoon dried egg

THIS IS WEEK 28—THE LAST OF RATION PERIOD NO. 7 (JAN 7TH TO FEB 3RD)

'What will she do to us now?'

A few potatoes can help to make a delicious dish—and I mean a few. It may be that you are short of potatoes, and, again, you might welcome a change from the usual boiled potato, which frankly, does not help to make a necessarily economical meal exciting. **Now don't think that 'making' dishes means making extra work.**
You will find that it does not take any longer to prepare the necessary additions than it would to prepare a large amount of potatoes.
The potato dumplings should be made with left-over potatoes and when you come to make them you have nothing to do but the mixing.

ROOT ROAST

This is more interesting than plain roast potatoes and will, therefore, do well with greens even if the meat is only a memory in the shape of dripping.
FOR TWO OR THREE HELPINGS—Clean two large parsnips, two or three medium carrots, one or two medium potatoes. You can add a thick slice of swede. Cut the roots into large chunks and mix.
Heat dripping in a baking tin and put the vegetable chunks

into it, fairly evenly. Put into a heated oven on the middle shelf and cook until soft. Halfway through the cooking time, toss the tin to turn the vegetables.

VEGETABLE STEW (3-4 persons)

INGREDIENTS—two parsnips, two or three onions, one swede (or three or four carrots), one potato, one rounded tablespoonful of dripping, seasoning. Curry powder optional.
Clean the vegetables and cut small. Heat the dripping in a fairly large saucepan. If you wish, add about one teaspoonful of curry and stir. Add the vegetables and salt and stir a few times over a brisk flame.
Cover the saucepan with a lid and simmer until the vegetables are soft, about 1/2—3/4hr.
Stir occasionally. Serve with freshly cooked greens.

EGG AND LEEK PIE

This egg and leek pie, made with cheese pastry, is an excellent solution to the main-dish problem, for dried eggs are a protein food, like meat.
If you have children in the house, serve dishes made with eggs often and make the most of this body-building food!
For this pie, you need: half a pound cheese pastry (made by substituting 2oz. grated cheese for 1oz. fat), half a pound of leeks (weight after preparing), seasoning, 4 dried eggs, reconstituted.
Divide the pastry into two and line the flat tin with one piece. Boil the leeks in salted water, drain and chop. Season and mix with eggs. (Dried eggs are easy to cook with, because whites and yolks are blended together). Pour into the pastry and cover with the second piece.
Bake in a hot oven for 30 minutes. (Sufficient for 4 people). Serve hot with vegetables, or cold with salad.

CORNED BEEF FRITTERS

Coat corned beef slices with batter and fry quickly in shallow hot fat.

CARTWHEEL PIES

Grease a fireproof dish and pour into it a fairly thick grave, about half an inch deep. Mix 6oz. plain flour with two rounded teaspoonfuls of baking powder, a pinch of salt and one level tablespoonful of dried egg (optional). Rub into this 1oz to 2oz. fat. (Or add finely chopped cooked fat removed from the joint). Wet this mixture with water or milk to a soft dough. Spoon portions into the gravy and fill the gaps with slices of corned beef and bake in a moderate oven for half an hour.

■ Hollywood is offering delegates to the San Francisco Conference on the United Nations a 'star delivery' service, which will save delegates from interrupting their conference activities to travel to Hollywood to meet their favourite star. The State Department declines the offer with thanks.
■ *The Water Carriers*, by Millet, sells in New York for $30,000 (£7,500).

21 Saturday

British fire pumps are rushed to Holland to fight **floods** after the Germans breech the Zuyder Zee dyke in two places. A quarter of the country is threatened and four million lives are at risk if the Germans breach any further dykes.
■ An all-party group of MPs visits the **Buchenwald** concentration camp at the invitation of General Eisenhower.
■ Names of new swimsuits on sale in New York—Strike Me Blue; Bandana Brief; Scanty Panties; Nappy Tied and Briefly Twisted.
FOOD FLASH: 22,680,000 shelled eggs have arrived from Canada. Torquay has received enough to give 6-10 on each ration book. Four other ships still at sea will raise the total to 600,000 boxes before the hot weather suspends shipments.

22 Sunday

The **milk ration** is raised to three pints a week.
■ **Leopold Stokowski** marries **Gloria Vanderbilt** in Mexico. They dash across the border and get married the day after she wins her divorce from Hollywood agent Pat di Cicco.
■ People who have managed to save money during the war are rushing to buy seaside **boarding houses**.

23 Monday
St George's Day

The **first British PoW**, WO George

Booth, who was shot down in the RAF's first raid on Wilhelmshaven on September 4, 1939, is released after 2,057 days in captivity.

■ For 33 years, a Washington society lady, Mary Woodward, lived with the **body** of her dead mother. Mrs Woodward had the body embalmed and used to visit it every day to commune with the dead woman's spirit.

24 Tuesday

Berlin almost completely **encircled** by Allied troops.

■ The San Francisco **conference** on the preparation of the United Nations Charter, which opens tomorrow, will be covered by 1,250 newspaper men of all nations.

■ It is announced that the **war** has **cost** £27,400 million to date.

25 Wednesday

Allied airmen will drop **food by parachute** to the starving people of north Holland. Eisenhower broadcasts a warning to the German garrisons not to interfere.

As soon as Holland is liberated, a special type of food, 'F Food', developed by the Medical Research Council, will be distributed. It is for cases of severe starvation, and in tests has restored patients so swiftly that within a few days they are ready for ordinary food.

■ **Marshal Pétain**, *left*, head of the Vichy government in France has asked permission for himself and his wife to cross from Switzerland to France to give himself up.

26 Thursday

It is anticipated that there will be a big rise in the **birth-rate** this year.

■ Collaboration charges against **Georges Simenon**, *right*, the Belgian detective story writer, are dropped because of insufficient evidence.

■ The Nazis agree to free **King Leopold** of the Belgians, and his family.

END OF THE TYRANTS

Just ten days after his 56th birthday, and with the Russian Army almost on the doorstep of the Reichs Chancellery, the Führer shoots himself. The body of Eva Braun, whom he had married the day before, is beside him. She had taken poison.

Mussolini and his mistress met their end, executed in Milan, just a week later. The Italian dictator was captured by partisans while lunching at Nesso.

27 Friday
Full moon

Mussolini is taken **prisoner** by partisans while having lunch at Nesso.

■ The complete foundations of a Roman building of the second and third centuries have been found on a blitzed site in Canterbury, Kent, also jewellery and pottery of outstanding importance.

■ Scottish **fishermen** have told their federation that as food is so precious, they want women on board to cook it.

28 Saturday

The Board of Trade announces that men will get a whole **handkerchief** per year.

■ The **birth-rate** last year was the highest since 1925—745,318 births. The infant

STRUNG UP: Mussolini and his mistress are hung and their bodies put on display in Milan. Below, the strutting dictator in uniform.

according to Dr R E G Armitage of the research centre of anthropology in Londonderry, who has just completed a study of the British Isles. His conclusions were read at a recent congress in Philadelphia.
■ Eleven **German generals** leave Euston station for a PoW camp somewhere in England

30 Monday

Humphrey Bogart announces his engagement to dazzling new star **Lauren Bacall**, *right*.
■ Over 600 tons of food is dropped on Holland by the RAF.
■ The first of 30,000 houses in crates arrive from the USA. Each house has two beds, a bathroom, kitchen and living room. The government intends to erect 145,000 of them.
■ **Snow** falls for five hours without a break in the Straits of Dover. There is 6ins of snow on the coast.

MAY

1 Tuesday

The **late frost** ruins the potato crop, the runner beans, peas, apples, plums and strawberries.
■ **France**, with women voting for the first time, swings left in the municipal elections.
■ American airmen are building the first **memorial** to the war— a playground at Freckleton, Lancs, where a bomber crashed on the village school.

mortality rate is 46 per thousand.
■ According to Moscow Radio, **Hermann Goering** has flown to an unknown destination with his wife, daughter and £5million-worth of money and valuables.
■ **Mussolini**, his mistress and 12 members of his cabinet are **executed**. Their bodies go on display in Milan.
■ Heaviest fall of **snow** for 50 years in the Dover Straits. Maximum temperature 46°F.

29 Sunday

The **Duke and Duchess of Windsor** attend service in the Anglican Cathedral in Nassau, and then broadcast a farewell to the people of the Bahamas.
■ **Brunettes** have a longer expectation of life than blondes, are more intelligent and manage their clothing coupons better,

2 Wednesday

Admiral Doenitz, *left*, announces the **death of Hitler** (on April 20th) and proclaims himself the new ruler of the Reich.
■ Italian hostilities cease.
■ All air-raid and lighting

restrictions are ended. To celebrate, the Savoy Hotel turns on all its lights and leaves its curtains undrawn.

■ **Pierre Laval**, *right,* the virtual head of the Vichy government and the most hated man in France, is **arrested** in Spain with his wife.

■ Another 800 tons of food is dropped on Holland.

. . . Dalwhinnie, Scotland is the coldest place in Britain tonight with the temperature 11°F below freezing. . .

3 Thursday

A million **Nazis surrender** in **Italy** and west **Austria**. **Berlin** surrenders.

■ All public **shelters** in the UK will be closed.

■ Mr P Cottrell, president of the Distributive and Allied Workers Federation, urges **women** to fight for **equality**.

■ British troops enter Rangoon.

4 Friday

Hamburg falls without a shot being fired while, in the Far East, Allied troops enter Rangoon after being given the all-clear by Wing Commander A E Saunders. The RAF officer noticed there was no activity when flying over the city. When he landed at the airfield he was told that the Japanese had left on April 25.

■ **Herbert Farjeon**, playwright and author, dies.

■ The **Big Four** (UK, USA, USSR and China) decide to invite France to their private meetings (The Big Five).

5 Saturday

8,000 Londoners are leaving the underground **shelters** after being given notice to quit. At the Elephant and Castle Mrs May Parsons (60) says, 'It's like being put out of your own home.'

■ All German forces in NW Germany, Holland and Denmark **surrender**.

■ Sir Giles Gilbert Scott's plans for the new **Coventry Cathedral** go on show at the Royal Academy.

6 Sunday

For the first time, large catches of **fish** landed at Grimsby this morning are sent on special fish trains to London, the southern counties and the southwest to be available for sale on Monday.

■ All civil prisoners will leave Dartmoor by end June/early July, to leave it free for Himmler, Doenitz, or other important Nazis, should they be captured.

■ **Fiorello la Guardia**, New York's most colourful mayor, whose nicknames include 'Manhattan Messiah' or 'Little Flower', announces that he will not run for re-election. During his years in office he has won a reputation for scrupulous honesty.

7 Monday

The new **German** foreign minister announces the **surrender** of all German fighting troops. The surrender document is signed at 2.41am by General Jodl in a schoolroom in Rheims, serving as Eisenhower's HQ.

THE NAZIS SURRENDER

At 2.41am on May 7, at General Eisenhower's HQ in Rheims, General Alfred Jodl, German Army Chief of Staff, signed the instrument of surrender, although the end had really come three days earlier when all the forces in NW Germany, Holland and Denmark were surrendered to Field Marshall Montgomery in his tent on Luneberg Heath.

■ Poet **Ezra Pound**, who broadcast propaganda from Italy to the USA throughout the war, is arrested in Genoa and will face an indictment for **treason**.

8 Tuesday

Germany surrenders—Mr **Churchill** announces the cessation of hostilities at one minute after midnight. Huge crowds gather in front of Buckingham Palace. The agreement signed at Rheims is ratified in Berlin— the signatories are Air Chief Marshal Tedder for Britain, Marshal Zhukov for the USSR, General de Lattre de Tassigny for France, and General Keitel for Germany.

■ **Goebbels** and his family are found **dead** in Berlin.

. . . Now the war is over the weather forecast is back. RACING: The 1,000 Guineas is won by Lord Derby's **Sunstream**, by 3/4 length from *Blue Smoke*.

9 Wednesday

King Leopold of the Belgians and his family, who have been held in custody in Salzburg by the Germans, are released.

■ **US troops** are starting to leave Europe. There are three million to go, at the rate of 250,000 to 300,000 per week.

■ **Goering** gives himself up to the Americans.

■ The German garrison on the Channel Islands surrenders.

■ The 2,000 Guineas is won by Lord Astor's **Court Martial**, who beats Sir Eric Ohlson's *Dante* by a neck.

10 Thursday

500 aircraft, some of them bombers, bring back 10,000 **PoWs**, and fly them over London.

■ 7,000 8th US Army Air Force ground crew men are flown on an air tour of the continent to see the **bomb damage**.

■ Many **wartime restrictions end**: the death penalty for looting is abolished, and sentries can no longer shoot to kill on the public highway. You can change your name without publishing it in the *London Gazette*,

VE DAY!

The war is over in the West

Jubilant crowds celebrate the end of war in Europe. 50,000 people go wild with joy, cheering Winston Churchill as he drives to lunch at the palace and, together with the royal family, makes eight appearances on the balcony. As dusk falls, the crowd moves to Piccadilly Circus to carry on the celebrations

and there can be more than one dog race per week.

■ The new **petrol allowance** will allow private persons to motor 150 miles a month.

■ **Family Allowances** Bill passes through the Commons—money will be paid to wives.

11 Friday
New Moon

Three days of revelling ends in only 10 cases of **drunkenness** at Bow Street.

■ There will be an extra 1lb of sugar for each ration book for **jam-making** in time for the soft fruit season.

■ Lt Col Burne (88), believed to be the last survivor of the defence of **Rorke's Drift** (immortalized in the film *Zulu*), died in Dorking yesterday.

...PHEW: It's 80°F in the shade today...

12 Saturday

Demob will begin on June 18.

Dutch Resistance men pick two baskets of strawberries in Holland and send them to Buckingham Palace and 10 Downing Street.

■ Drivers are asked to treat the restoration of a petrol ration with respect. Children are not used to motor traffic. Also, cars that have been laid up for years can be lethal.

■ The atmospheric **balloons** that helped win the war will now help spy the weather in advance, and produce more accurate weather forecasts.

FOOD FLASH: **Apricot jam** soon—the Ministry of Food has bought 9,250 tons of apricot pulp from Spain.

13 Sunday

Thanksgiving service at St Paul's. The King, the Queen, the two princesses, Queen Mary, King Haakon of Norway, Queen Wilhelmina of the Netherlands, King Peter of Yugoslavia and the President of Poland are among those present, as well as Winston Churchill, *left*.

■ Some of Britain's greatest art treasures are back at the National Gallery, visited by the King and Queen, *left*. In the first batch are Titian's *Bacchus and Ariadne*, Van Eyck's *Jean Arnolfini*, Hobbema's *The Avenue*, and Rembrandt's self-portrait.

■ **Crown Prince Olaf** returns to Norway. He crosses the North Sea in a British cruiser accompanied by 15 other British and Norwegian ships. Minesweepers have cleared the Skagerrak and Oslo Fjord of German mines. The only Germans left in Norway are naval personnel waiting to hand over their warships.

...Temperature in London 79°F at midday, dropping 13°F by 7p.m...

14 Monday

There is a serious shortage of civilian **clothes** for the men and women about to be demobilised, because of the lack of cloth and workers.

■ Two weeks' food is landed on the Channel Islands (2,000 tons).

■ There is a **wedding boom** in Warrington as US flyers are posted to the Far East. There are between 5-12 marriages a day.

■ Hundreds of sappers are on the **beaches** clearing the **mines**, so that Britain's war workers can enjoy a seaside holiday.

15 Tuesday

Field Marshal **Montgomery** opens an exhibition in Paris designed to give the French a chance to bring their knowledge of Britain up to date. It includes a captured VI flying bomb, and shows how AA batteries, fighter aircraft and balloon men destroyed 3,739 buzz bombs in 80 days. It also shows the other theatres of war where the UK fought after the fall of France, and where the war against the Japanese is still being fought.

■ The *Sunbeam II*—the first drifter released after five years with the Royal Navy - sets out from Lowestoft for the herring fishing grounds of Scotland.

■ So much **fish** is arriving in Grimsby that the ports cannot handle it.14,000 boxes have been landed, and 70 ships—51 of them Danish—are waiting to be unloaded.

16 Wednesday

Heber Jebdiah Grant (88), the sixth president of the **Mormons** after Brigham Young, dies in Salt Lake City.

■ An Allied **Military** Government will run Germany.

■ Mr Churchill reveals to the House of Commons that the **King** had a tommygun and used to practise in the garden of Buckingham Palace. He added that if it had come to a last stand in London, he was quite sure the King would have been prepared to use it, ignoring the advice of his ministers.

■ Thanksgiving Service at St Giles Cathedral, Edinburgh, attended by the King, the Queen, and the two princesses.

17 Thursday

The **Sunderland Flying Boat**, *above,* is unveiled. It can carry 70 passengers with a cruising speed of 184mph and has a range of 4,650 miles. In the new summer schedules BOAC will make four flights a day every week until winter. The trip from Poole, Dorset to Baltimore is 3,724 miles, with one stop in Newfoundland. It will take 30 hours. This new service is in addition to the North Atlantic landplane service which flies daily in

both directions between Prestwick, Scotland and Montreal, Canada.

18 Friday

Eamon de Valera, the prime minister of Eire, says that the Irish government will send £3 million of clothing and food to Europe.

■ Goering, Doenitz, Kesselring, Rundstedt and other prominent **Nazi war criminals** are being moved to selected places of incarceration to await trial.

■ **Frost** has taken such a heavy toll of soft fruit this year that the growers are asking the Ministry of Food for a rise in the prices they can charge—two-thirds of the gooseberry crop and 25-50% of the strawberry crop has been wiped out .

19 Saturday

■ A father and three of his sons will contest the next General Election in Britain. They are: **Isaac Foot**, *right,* member for S.E. Cornwall and Liberal candidate for Tavistock, Devon; Dingle Foot, Liberal member for Dundee; John Foot, Liberal candidate for S.E. Cornwall, and Michael Foot, Labour candidate for Devonport.

■ A 50-car train loaded with **Hungarian gold** bullion, jewellery, rare furniture and valuable rugs, estimated to be worth millions, has been found hidden in a tunnel in the little town of Buchstein by the US 7th Army. The train was sent out by the Hungarian finance minister to stop it falling into the hands of the Red Army, only to fall to the Americans.

■ Two girls (16), who broke into **Frank Sinatra**'s house, took several large bundles tied with blue ribbon only to find it was fan mail saved for Sinatra.

20 Sunday

Whitsun

Whitsun holiday washed out by rain. The Victoria Pavilion on Folkestone Pier, is destroyed by fire.

■ Denmark says it is ready to feed Europe. Its agricultural economy is virtually intact.

21 Monday
Whit Monday

Now that the defensive shore-barriers have been removed, **beaches** are open to the public again.

■ The Standard Car Company announces that it will concentrate on two models, the **Standard 8**, *right,* and the Standard 12. For the first time, the eight will have a four-speed gearbox with syncromesh in top, third and second gears. The postwar 12 will be 3ins wider and the front seats are adjustable for height and leg reach. New cars will cost 50% -60% more than pre-war prices when the Standard 8 was £135 and the Standard 12 was £225.

■ The secretary of the British Empire Games Committee suggests that the **Olympic Games** should be revived and held in **London** in either 1948 or 1952.

■ Winston Churchill proposes that the **coalition** government should continue until the defeat of Japan. The Labour Party elects to withdraw from the coalition and calls for a general election.

22 Tuesday

Labour want more **women candidates**. Only 25 were chosen to stand in the last election.

■ When a record fish catch looked like going bad because there was no road or rail transport available, the Russians flew 112,500lbs of fish from the Caspian Sea to canning factories. The result, as some of the fish were sturgeon, was **caviar** as well.

■ A Russian professor who **transplants** frogs' hearts, has succeeded in grafting a second heart onto a warm-blooded animal.

23 Wednesday

More cuts in rations. Meat is raised to 1s.2d. worth per week, but must include more corned beef. Bacon is 3ozs per week. Cheese is expected to remain at 2ozs per week. No more clothing coupons until

HOLIDAYS ARE BACK—BUT THERE'S A QUEUE TO GET AWAY!

September.

■ Field Marshal **Montgomery** is appointed commander-in-chief of the British Occupation Forces and Allied Control Commission in Germany.

■ The **coalition** government **ends**. Mr Churchill hands his resignation to the King, and forms a caretaker government. The General Election will be on July 5.

24 Thursday

Roses, tulips and lupins, grown in the back gardens of Bristol and Avonmouth docks, are decorating the wards of hospital ships taking US wounded home. Docker Bill Thorne spotted a US nurse picking buttercups in a waste patch near the dockyard. 'After what they've done for us, we can give them something better than that,' he said, and he and his mates are doing just that.

■ The King and Queen give an **Empire Day party** at Buckingham Palace for ex-PoWs.

25 Friday

News has leaked out that **Heinrich Himmler**, head of the SS, killed himself with a phial of **cyanide** in the HQ of the 2nd British Army on Wednesday night (May 23). He had been picked up by British troops near Hanover on Monday. They took him to a camp near the British HQ where he revealed his identity to the commandant. A doctor examined him for hidden poison and, as he asked him to open his mouth, he bit quickly on the phial.

■ Death of Mr Thomas Booth of Kingsway, Boston, Lincs, the last man in Britain to grow and process woad, formerly used to dye police and postmen's uniforms.

26 Saturday

Because of the shortage of **teachers**, local authorities are asking retired teachers to stay on.

■ Churchill opens the election campaign.

■ High-legged **boots** which could be turned into shoes saved many airmen's lives. British boot designers produced a boot which became a shoe when the high leg was cut off. A knife was supplied hidden in the lining.

27 Sunday
Full moon

The crew of the RAF research plane Aries have discovered a 100 year-old error in the position of the **North magnetic pole**, which shows that the pole is 200-300 miles away from where it was determined by J C Ross on June 1, 1831, on the Boothia Peninsula, the most northerly Canadian mainland territory. Aries fixed the pole in the Sverdrup Islands, 1,500 miles from the geographical North pole.

28 Monday

William Joyce, alias **Lord Haw Haw** ('Jairmany calling'), *left*, whose propaganda broadcasts from Germany throughout the war amused and infuriated millions in equal parts, is wounded and **captured** near the Danish border, left.

■ The Chief Keeper of the Brussels Art **museum** returns from Austria with the Van Eyck painting *L'Agneau Mystique*, which had been delivered to Hitler, and kept in a salt-mine in Alt Aussee in Austria.

29 Tuesday

Kippers are back in the shops, at 10d. a lb. Though fish is in short supply, 14,000 boxes are stuck on the dock at Grimsby because of zoning regulations.

■ The convoy system is ended for ships in non-combat zones.

30 Wednesday

Scientists at the Torrey Research Station, Aberdeen, have discovered how to quick-freeze fish so that it keeps for a year. Now it is only a question of getting quick-freeze developed on a commercial scale.
■ Children are leaving **school** earlier to go to work. Board of Education statistics show a falling-off of 14 year-old children in school.
■ **Knut Hamsen**, the Norwegian Nobel laureate, and his wife, are put under house detention on charges of collaboration.

31 Thursday

Soviet architects have designed a 2-3-roomed cottage for amateurs - homeless people who want to build themselves a home. The government provides materials and money to help.
■ **Humphrey Bogart** marries **Lauren Bacall** in Hollywood, *left*.
■ The manuscript of *The Eustace Diamonds* by Anthony Trollope is sold at Sotheby's for £540.

JUNE

1 Friday

General **Dwight D. Eisenhower**, Supreme Commander Allied Powers in Europe, is given the Freedom of the City of London.
■ Grandmothers of nearly 70 and girls of 18 are among the two teams of 12 women navvies helping to clean up the **ruins** of Plymouth. They earn £2.18s. for a 44-hour week.
■ Everton footballer **Tommy Lawton**, *right*, asks to be placed on the transfer list as his wife wants to move south for health reasons.

2 Saturday

Queen Mary returns to Marlborough House from her wartime home at Badminton.

MY KIND OF TOWN! General Eisenhower is given the Freedom of the City of London

■ **Anthony Eden**, the Foreign Secretary, has a duodenal ulcer, and Winston Churchill takes over the job.
■ There is a **bread crisis** in London—not enough bakers.
... AGNES BADEN POWELL (87), the founder of the Girl Guides, dies. . .

3 Sunday

A motor freighter, sailing far south of the shipping route from the Cape to South America, encountered thousands of **whales**, 400 miles to the east of Tristan da Cunha Island, feeding on white sea anemones. The vessel steamed amongst them for 100 miles.
■ The British **General Election** campaign opens. Churchill broadcasts for 20mins after the BBC Nine O'clock News, on behalf of the Conservative party.

4 Monday

A vast **hoard of money** has been found buried beneath the floorboards of a barn near Berchtesgaden. It was Himmler's 'little nest egg'. Among the currency was £26,000. In all, the currency of 26 nations was represented.
■ Four RAF **Mosquitoes** fly from the UK to India in under 13 hours.

5 Tuesday

Britain's secret fighter squadron is to be deployed against the Japanese. The 25 members are peregrine **falcons** trained to blitz enemy information-carrying pigeons. The squadron first went into action when the UK authorities became worried by the amount of information travelling out of this country by carrier pigeon.

■ Joint declaration on **Berlin** by the four Allied commanders—Germany will be divided into **four occupied zones**, and Berlin into four demarcation zones

■ Planeloads of ATS arrive in Hamburg, to be greeted by cheering troops, fed up with the non-fraternization rules.

6 Wednesday

■ Because of the shortage of shoe leather, **Perugio's** of the Rue de la Paix, Paris, is making summer shoes out of old fire hoses.

■ Priceless literary and art **treasures** are removed from their wartime hiding place in a tunnel near Aberystwyth. When they were put there in 1939, none of the villagers knew that the boxes contained treasures like the *Codex Sinaiticus*. Treasures returned to the National Library of Scotland from an English chalk cave and three border strongholds, include Sir Walter Scott's manuscripts and letters, including the last one written by Mary Queen of Scots.

7 Thursday

The Australian Federation of Commercial Broadcasting Stations say that much of the material purchased from the BBC is unacceptable because of **questionable jokes**. The worst offenders are Tommy Trinder, Max Miller and Tommy Handley.

■ **German PoWs** lay carpets in the streets of the Channel Islands for a visit by the King and Queen. It is the Queen's first flight by air since she became Queen.

■ **King Haakon,** *left,* returns to Norway to an emotional welcome from the Norwegian people, five years exactly to the day he and his government left to carry on the fight from England.

■ The **Big Five** agree on the right of veto in the UN council.

... Sadler's Wells reopens with the first performance of Benjamin Britten's *Peter Grimes...*

8 Friday

The war, from invasion to victory, has cost 547 Canadian and British troops a day. US

JANE

In emptying barracks all over the world pictures of neglected lovelies are slowly peeling from the walls.... doing their last strip as it were!

WHOOPEE!— "I'M ON MY WAY OUT" AT LAST, GINGER!

LUCKY TWERP!— LEAVE US YOUR ART GALLERY!

Jane, alone in her new-found flat in civvy-street, asks herself...

WHAT IS THE FUTURE OF A PIN-UP GIRL?

ground forces lost 1,527 per day (Army only).
■ Because there is such a shortage of **schoolteachers**, those in the forces will be demobbed quickly.
■ The first post-war Oaks, at Newmarket, is won by Lord Derby's **Sun Stream**, ridden by **Harry Wragg**.

9 Saturday

Derby Day: a horse that cost just £15.15s. runs in the Derby today,the 100-1 outsider *Audentes*. But the race is won by the favourite, Sir Eric Ohlson's **Dante**.
■ 800 church bells, taken by the Germans from Holland and Belgium, have been found in a metal foundry in Hamburg.

10 Sunday
New moon

The King takes the salute at the Civil Defence and Allied Services farewell parade in Hyde Park led by Peter, a Scottish collie and Animal VC.
■ Marshal Zhukov bestows Russia's Order of Victory on his fellow military commanders, General Eisenhower and Field Marshal Montgomery in Frankfurt. The Order is a glittering star, each one set with 99 diamonds and rubies, and valued at £4,000 apiece. (Eisenhower and Montgomery are the first non-Russians ever to receive it.)
■ When **Dante** the Derby winner returned to Middleham, Yorks, hundreds of people from all parts of Yorkshire, many of whom had bets of long standing at 12 to 1, had come to greet him. They sang 'Cock of the North' as he walked from his box.

11 Monday

Allies are pushing ever harder against Japan. **General MacArthur** leads assault groups on British North Borneo.
■ RAF heavy **bombers** have launched an all-out attack on the millions of flies and mosquitoes infesting Rangoon. Flying at little more than roof height, they spray the city with DDT. These spray bombers have made thousands of square miles safe from many diseases.

DAD'S HOME!

Planes and boats trains bring the fi[ght]ing men and priso[n]ers of war back h[ome] to their families. I[n] some cases, like t[he] one in Torquay, below, the whole street turned out [to] welcome back one [of] the neighbours . . .

JUNE

■ **Lord Haw Haw** (see May 28) is flown to Brussels. He will eventually be flown to Britain to stand trial for high treason.
■ The German ambassador to **Tokyo** has been told by the Japanese that they consider his mission at an end.
■ **Cigarettes** are the best currency in Germany. A packet has the purchasing power of £1. Tea, coffee and soap are susbsidiary currencies.

12 Tuesday

78 US ships are sunk or damaged off **Okinawa**, their greatest number of losses in any single campaign. Japanese **suicide planes** attack continuously *(left)*.
■ **General Eisenhower** is invested with an honorary OM at Buckingham Palace.
■ In 1940, Mr Jack Commins of Plymouth posted a **letter** and ten £1 notes to his son serving aboard *HMS Arethusa* in the Mediterranean. The letter never arrived. Yesterday, the letter was returned to Mr. Commins by the post office marked 'Detained in France during the German Occupation'. The £10 was still inside.
■ Raising the school-leaving age will increase the number of school children to 390,000, says the new Minister of **Education,** Mr Law.
■ Mr Stephen Denton of Sandal, nr. Wakefield, Yorks, on a business trip to London, left £445.10s. in a cardboard box fastened with sellotape, in a taxi cab. The next passenger took it to the police, who returned it to Mr Denton.

13 Wednesday

World Amateur **Jive** Championship at Wembley Town Hall. The winners were Sonia Rudnick (18) of London, and LAC Lloyd Lindemann of Toronto. Lloyd was wearing jive trousers for the occasion with 17ins bottoms and 28ins knees.
■ The British Army **football** team, *pictured*

above, has returned to Italy after touring the Middle East with an unbeaten record of played 10, won nine and drew one. Led by **Matt Busby**, *front right*, the Scottish half-back, they scored 55 goals against 10. The troops have asked for more such games.
■ Australian troops in Borneo capture **Brunei**.
■ Offices and shops close for two hours in Mettar, Georgia, USA, so that the residents can pray for rain to break the drought menacing their tobacco and corn crops.

14 Thursday

The National **Farmers** Union say that Britain faces the most frugal rations in living

THE HIT SONGS OF 1945

Memorable melodies from Donald Peers (far left), Frank Sinatra and Doris Day.

JANUARY
Come Out, Come Out Wherever You Are
Geraldo & his Orchestra with Les Cabon
You, Fascinating You
Donald Peers
She Broke My Heart in Three Places
The Hoosier Hot Shots
Dream   *Frank Sinatra*
FEBRUARY
Just a Little Fond Affection
Joe Loss & his Orchestra with Elizabeth Batey
MARCH
Can't Help Singing
Deanna Durbin
My Dreams are Getting Better
Lou Praeger & his Orchestra
Pretty Kitty Blue Eyes
The Merry Macs
There Goes That Song Again
Russ Morgan
APRIL
Love is My Reason (Ivor Novello) *Muriel Barron*
Gonna Build a Big Fence Around Texas
Eric Winstone & his Orchestra with Alan Kane
Suddenly it's Spring
Hildegard
MAY
Don't Fence Me In
Bing Crosby & the Andrews Sisters
Everytime We Say Goodbye
Ella Fitzgerald
A Little on the Lonely Side
Geraldo & his Orchestra

JUNE
Ac-cent-tchu-ate the Positive
Bing Crosby
We'll Gather Lilacs
Olive Gilbert & Muriel Barron
JULY
The Cokey Cokey (also known as the Hokey Cokey by
Lou Praeger & his Orchestra) *Paul Rich*
I'm Beginning to See the Light
Duke Ellington & his Orchestra
Saturday Night is the Loneliest Night of the Week
Frank Sinatra
AUGUST
Chewing a Piece of Straw
Jack Payne & the Crackerjacks
Laura   *Dick Haymes*
One Meat Ball
The Andrews Sisters
SEPTEMBER
The More I See You
Dick Haymes
There I've Said It Again
Vaughn Monroe
OCTOBER
Bell BottomTrousers
Jack Payne & his Orchestra
Let Him Go, Let Him Tarry
Evelyn Knight & the Jesters
NOVEMBER
I'm in Love with Two Sweethearts
Issy Bon
DECEMBER
Sentimental Journey   *Doris Day*

memory next winter because of insufficient skilled labour. The NFU has asked the government to give priority release to farmers' sons and farm workers.

■ The War Office says that if **ATS girls** wish to wear their greatcoats after demob it will cost them 30s. If they want to get their money back, they can take the greatcoat, labelled and tied with string, to any railway station and the 30s. will be refunded by the railway company.

■ The King appoints **Marshal Zhukov** of the USSR an honorary Grand Knight of the Most Honourable Order of the Bath (Military Division) in recognition of his great services to the Allied cause.

■ All **British PoWs liberated** by the Western Allies are now home.

■ Hong Kong burns after 25,000 gallons of jellied petrol is dropped on it.

15 Friday

Jawarhalal Nehru, *left,* and seven other detained members of the Indian Congress Party are released as a first step towards increased self-government in India.

■ The All-England Lawn **Tennis** Club, at Wimbledon, a driving school for firemen since 1942, has been derequisitioned, and the No 1 Court will be used for the Interservice games on June 30, and the British v the Allies match on June 28. The Centre Court cannot be used because of bomb damage.

■ **Berlin** is selected as the venue for the Big Three **Conference** between President Truman, Mr Churchill and Marshal Stalin. Mr Attlee will accompany Mr Churchill as he may well be elected to govern the country after the election. 597 Labour candidates will stand in the general election, 40 of whom are women.

16 Saturday

von Ribbentrop, *left,* is arrested in a Hamburg boarding house where he has been hiding for six weeks. He had with him three letters addressed to 'Vincent' Churchill, Field Marshal Montgomery and Mr Eden. He had hoped to remain at large until British feeling against Germany had died down and then surrender. News of his arrest has been kept quiet for several days.

■ The military authorities in Germany have given the Bremen Symphony Orchestra permission to rehearse, but Jewish composers such as Mendelssohn, Mahler, Offenbach and others must be included in the programmes.

■ The professional secrets of **Harry Houdini**, the great escapologist, are lost for ever with the death of his brother in New York. When Houdini died in 1926, he asked that all his equipment and secrets be destroyed when his brother died.

17 Sunday

St James's Hospital, Leeds, is appealing for help from any public-spirited women with experience of cooking in an institution, hotel, or large house, or it may have to close down. The hospital has only one assistant cook, a girl of 18, assisted by a handful of maids, to produce meals for 1,000 patients and nursing staff. Now the girl has decided to leave.

■ What may be the **lost treasure** of Hernando **Cortes**, the 16th century Spanish conqueror of Mexico, has been found in a deep cave near Amecameca, southeast of Mexico City. Eight hikers found 15 boxes filled with gold and precious stones, apparently Indian in origin and of rare quality.

18 Monday

There is a threat to **assassinate** the Duke and Duchess of Gloucester on their tour of Queensland.

BUCK RYAN

William Joyce, (Lord Haw Haw), is being held in Bow Street police station. He is in cell number six, once occupied by Crippen. The door is never closed, policemen are always on watch, and the station yard is floodlit at night. He will face charges of high treason today.

■ It is one of the worst seasons ever for soft fruit. The **crops** have been **ruined** by May frosts and heavy rains since.

■ King Leopold of the Belgians, who is still living near Salzburg with his wife and family, is warned not to return to Belgium until and unless the government send for him.

19 Tuesday

Thousands of Britain's servicemen and women step out of the ranks for the last time amid tears and flowers. In beaming batches of 30, they go through their last bit of Army discipline. There are no **demob** suits for servicewomen.

■ The first **evacuees** return this week when 1,271 mothers and children arrive in London.

■ The **Big Three** meeting in Berlin draw up the master plan to run the Reich.

■ The £235,000 million spent on the war would have given everyone in the world £125.

■ Belgian's Liberal party calls on King Leopold to abdicate.

. . . The start of Britain's first peacetime HEATWAVE.

20 Wednesday

King Leopold refuses to abdicate. His brother continues to act as regent, and it is unlikely that the King will ever return.

■ Charlecote Park, nr. Stratford-on-Avon, and Flint Cottage, Box Hill, Surrey, the home of George Meredith for 40 years, have been presented to the National Trust.

■ St James's Hospital, Leeds will stay open as ATS girls awaiting demob, housewives, and canteen assistants all come to the rescue. The hospital is being run on almost normal lines.

■ Australian troops land on **Sarawak**.

21 Thursday

Mushrooms by the ton may soon be coming to Britain from the Channel Islands, grown in the vast concrete-lined tunnels which slave workers constructed for the Germans. All that was required to turn them into the world's biggest mushroom farm was a layer of compost in which to plant the mushroom spore.

■ £1,000 million of **treasure** found in the vaults of the Reichsbank in Regensburg is the main national wealth of Austria and Bavaria.

■ The Royal Netherlands Navy will provide the Royal Naval Colleges at Dartmouth and

Greenwich with **Dutch bulbs** each spring as a token of gratitude for the hospitality and friendship experienced during the war.

22 Friday

Battle of **Okinawa,** *right,* is won after 82 days. The Japanese lost 90,000 men.
■ The Italian premier, Signor Parri, announces that Italy is to become a Republic.
■ Leaders of the Belgian Catholic party inform the prime minister that they have decided to form a government under King Leopold.
■ The Adjutant General of the Forces says he was astonished to see British privates in Italy queuing to pay £1 for a seat at the **opera**. He said the Army had trained 115,000 illiterate men to read and write.

23 Saturday

The *Winged Victory* is back in the Louvre after her wartime sojourn in a stable. So are the *Venus de Milo* and the *Mona Lisa*.
■ A rush of Germans wanting to get Nazi and **SS tattoo marks** erased has led to German doctors being forbidden to perform such operations.
■ Leaders of the Tyneside **shipyards** and engineering works warn the government of serious strikes if there is no improvement in the food position in northern industrial towns.

24 Sunday

15,000 **GIs leave** for the USA on the *Queen Elizabeth, left*. Since she began her life as a war transport, the *Queen Elizabeth* has completed 36 round trips of the North Atlantic, and has carried more than 600,000 persons. Together with the *Queen Mary*, the two ships have carried 1,250,000 fighting men.
■ Trippers pour to the beaches, and many end up spending the night there. Trains are so packed that crowds of people are left behind at Brighton and Southend. At 10pm the temperature is still 74°F.

25 Monday
Full moon

Thousands of babies in Europe suffering from **rickets** due to bad feeding can be cured with a single massive dose of Vitamin D2, writes Dr David Krestin in *The Lancet*.
■ Among **Hungarian treasures** found in Salzburg, Austria, was the hand of St Stephen, over 1,000 years old, and the Hungarian crown.
■ **Hassan Ali** (90) dies in Khartoum. He had been General Gordon's servant.

26 Tuesday

Angry women mob two **girls undressing** on the beach at Brighton for a bathe, complaining that the girls are making a spectacle of themselves, and that it is positively embarrassing.
■ Dutch radio says that 85% of the country **flooded** by the Germans has already been drained, and the soil has dried so quickly that

sowing has already taken place.

27 Wednesday

The **tea ration** is to be increased by 1/2oz to 2 1/2oz per person per week from July 22.

■ For three days it has been **freezing** in Johannesburg. It's the coldest June in S Africa for 12 years.

■ The Allied **invasion fleet** is 100 miles from the coast of Japan.

■ 151 delegates queue for eight hours to sign the United Nations Charter in San Francisco.

28 Thursday

Because so many farm workers are still in the services, 65,000 volunteers are needed to save the **potato harvest**.

■ When Red Army girls are demobbed they are given a woollen or silk dress, two sets of underwear, a pair of high-heeled shoes, and two pairs of stockings.

■ **Oswald Mosley**, leader of the British Fascist Party, says he has no intention of being active in politics again, and that now his only interests are books and farming.

29 Friday

Bosco, a cross between a collie and a spitz, walked 2,300 miles to be reunited with his owner. He was sent from Knoxville, Tennessee, to Glendale, California, to be met there by Mrs Flanagan and her son Paul when they arrived on a visit. When they went to collect him, they found a crate with a hole. They offered a reward for Bosco's return, but heard nothing, and eventually returned to Tennessee. They subsequently moved house. Seven months later, Mrs Flanagan passed her old house and saw a skinny dog on the steps. It was Bosco. He had walked over mountains, across deserts, through swamps

and along dusty roads crowded with traffic. After a good meal, Bosco fell asleep in his favourite position— all four legs in the air.

30 Saturday

Gainsborough Pictures of Shepherds Bush, London, launch a scheme whereby any ATS, WRAF or WRN may borrow/hire a wedding or bridesmaid's dress actually worn on the screen. They can choose from a white satin gown worn by Anne Shelton in Waterloo Road, a cobwebby net worn by **Margaret Lockwood**, *left*, when she starred in *Love Story*, or an oyster satin dress worn by **Dulcie Gray** in *They Were Sisters*. The dresses may be kept for three days, and Gainsborough Pictures will do alterations.

■ **Queen Mary**, *below*, is at Wimbledon to see the US Services lawn tennis team beat the British Empire Services team 4-1 on No 1 Court.

JULY

1 Sunday

Dominion Day, Canada

A **whirlwind** tears through Folkestone, ripping the roof off the cinema, uprooting trees, blowing in windows, and overturning sheds and garages.

■ Work has begun on the largest plane to be built in Britain, the **Brabazon 1**, a 110-ton airiner, which will carry 72 passengers 3,000 miles. The lounge in the

centre of the top deck is 30ft long, and the width of the plane. Between the pilots and the lounge is accommodation for 38 passengers in armchairs, which convert into berths for the night. The wingspan is 230ft.

2 Monday

W H Weeks (51) of St Ives, Cornwall, and his son Geoffrey (19), who left home months ago to pick up their 10-ton yacht *Susannah,* which had been laid up for the war at Lelant Estuary, are picked up off the Canary Islands by an RN harbour craft. The yacht was in an unsailable condition, and Mr Weeks and his son had been badly injured in a storm.

■ **Paris fashion** prices shock. A pink-and-white imitation linen suit costs £85 plus tax at 40%; a green-and-white rayon print frock costs £62.10s. plus 40% tax.

3 Tuesday

The General Election: Both parties have campaigned on the same lines: to use the resources of the country to provide food, homes and jobs for all, and insurance against the hazards of ill-fortune, sickness and old age.

4 Wednesday

The **Japanese** begin the evacuation of Japanese citizens from Java.
■ British troops, led by the **Desert Rats**, enter Berlin, watched by glum-faced Germans.
■ The Shawfield Greyhound racing track, Glasgow, installs the first camera to photograph close finishes from the correct angle. Wembley will follow.

5 Thursday
Polling Day

Twenty people are taken to hospital when a large portion of the 100-foot-high ceiling of the Theatre Royal, St

Helens, Lancs, crashes on the stalls, pit and circle.
■ The British and Norwegian governments are to extend next winter's whaling season in view of the world shortage of fats, and hope to get 500,000 barrels of oil.
■ The King and Queen arrive on the Isle of Man, where the King opens the **Tynwald** for the first time in British history.

6 Friday

A secret weapon aimed at livening up the local is about to be launched. It is a Super-Toned **Juke Box**. Mr T Murphy, secretary of the Showman's Guild, predicts a big future for the juke box in the UK.
■ **Stalin,** *left,* receives Dr Hewlett-Johnson, Dean of Canterbury, in the Kremlin.

. . . **30,000 cases of frozen rabbits arrive in London from Australia . . .**

7 Saturday

Food **rations** for British troops in the Mediterranean have been **reduced** to release more food for their families in Britain.
■ **Synthetic rubber** golf and tennis balls will be made soon in limited numbers.
■ Lord Rosebery's *Ocean Swell,* becomes the first Derby winner since 1897 to go on to win the **Ascot Gold Cup**, when he beats

"This iss terrible! — we're going to get a fair trial!"

the favourite, *Teheran*, ridden by Gordon Richards. Sir Eric Ohlson, owner of this year's Derby winner *Dante*, turns down an offer of £90,000 for his horse.

8 Sunday

Great crowds take to the Thames at the **Henley regatta**.

■ The last **Halifax** bomber, *above*, to be produced at the Rootes factory in Speke will be rolled out of the factory tomorrow. The aircraft workers have placed a grave on the tarmac which reads, 'Installed in memory of John Halifax, who died June 15, 1945.'

9 Monday
New moon

Mr Robert Firman, managing director of Caledonian Fish Selling Company, hopes that grilled kipper stands will soon be found on fair and pleasure grounds all over the country.

■ **Stud fees** for *Nearco*, the sire of the Derby winner **Dante**, rocket to £4,830 for 1946, bringing his possible earnings for a full season to £138,000. The previous highest record was 1,890gns for the National Stud stallion *Big Game*—the best-guarded horse in Britain during the war. Every night he was trotted into a specially-built £500 air-raid shelter.

■ There is a **partial eclipse** of the sun today, visible from northern parts of the country.

10 Tuesday

The woad farm at Boston, Lincs, last surviving relic of a once prosperous industry, is to be bought by the town council for a housing estate.

■ Corporal Margaret Hastings, a WAC in the US army, and two companions are rescued after 46 days in the hidden valley of 'Shangri-La', in the Orange Mountains of New Guinea. The valley is ruled by a painted queen with a harem of 15 men. They are the only survivors of a US transport plane that crashed in May.

11 Wednesday

Oklahoma farmers are dumping their bumper grain crop, because the railways cannot transport it.

■ The problems over feeding and fuelling **Berlin** are sorted out. The Allies are taking 15-day turns to run the city. Each of the four military commanders will serve in rotation, and the capital will be fed and fuelled by pooling resources from all the occupation zones.

■ **Japan** is **bombarded** by 1,000 planes of the US task force.

■ Police are called to disperse a queue of 75 angry women outside a dairy in Palmers Green, London, when after waiting 1 1/2hrs for ice cream they were told it had all been ordered. Housewives are setting up an Anti-Queue Campaign.

12 Thursday

Britain's ace 'secret service squadron' of **carrier pigeons** (40 birds trained to bring back information from Europe's

underground during the war), *left*, will be flown to Berlin on Saturday to race back over 600 miles with the first messages from the Big Three conference. Among the pigeons are those which brought the news of the flying bomb sites in the Pas de Calais, and the one VC pigeon of the war which brought a message of 5,000 words and sketch plans and maps of the fortifications of France just before D Day.

■ Prince Charles, the Belgian regent, accompanied by the presidents of both houses of parliament, is flying to Salzburg to see his brother King Leopold.

13 Friday

The UK is to receive 250 million lbs of **meat** from the USA in the last quarter of the year, which means that there is unlikely to be a cut in the meat ration. Europe's crop of **wheat** is expected to be the lowest since 1939.

■ The Army are to get fewer **cigarettes**— the weekly NAAFI ration is to be cut from 75 to 60 per person.

14 Saturday

Thousands of **motorists** who licenced their cars on June I cannot get them on the road because of the shortage of batteries, and the difficulty of getting old batteries replated. Some garages have been told they will have to wait eight months for new batteries, and five months for replated ones.

■ Cigarettes which explode when they are half-smoked are among the **booby traps** left behind by the Japanese in Burma.

15 Sunday

Masonry and glass from **Bath Abbey** and five of Bath's churches, bombed during Baedeker and other raids on the city, is being sent to Lakeview, Ontario, for incorporation in a new church there.

... The HOTTEST day of the year. A temperature of 90°F is recorded in Norwich...

16 Monday

King Leopold refuses to give up his throne and tells the Belgian caretaker government that he is not returning from Salzburg.

■ The **housing shortage** is worsening. The Federation of Building Trades Employers, which has been pushing for more men since VE-day, say that unless they get more workers the soldiers will have no

WOODCOCK'S CROWN

Bruce Woodcock and his fiancee celebrate his British and Empire Heavyweight title success against Jack London at White Hart Lane (right)

homes to come back to. Local authorities say they can use all the German PoWs they can get.

17 Tuesday

A huge Allied **fleet**, the most powerful naval force ever assembled in the Pacific, is **shelling Tokyo**. The attacks opened at dawn yesterday, and are still continuing. Nearly 500 Super Fortresses drop more than 2,500 **fire bombs** on four Japanese cities —Numazu, Kuwana, Oita, and Heratsuka.

■ France is thinking of scrapping the **guillotine**, and has asked the US government for information on more humane methods of execution.

■ **Bruce Woodcock**, a 24-year-old Doncaster railwayman, knocks out **Jack London** in the sixth round at Wembley to

■ Italy and Austria are again connected by the **Brenner railway** line.
■ William (Lord Haw-Haw) Joyce's lawyer applies for a postponement of his trial as documents vital to the defence have not yet arrived in this country.

19 Thursday

Brighton Town Council passes a resolution to demand power from the Health Ministry to requisition **empty houses** for distressed families of servicemen and civilians.
■ 250 Belgian girls arrive in Britain as **volunteers** for domestic work in hard-pressed British hospitals.
■ William (Lord Haw-Haw) Joyce's trial is postponed until September. His major defence is that as he was born in the USA, he cannot owe allegiance to the British Crown.
■ Lincoln **bombers** will soon be in operation in Japan. They have a range of 3,000 miles, and can carry a bomb load of more than 10 tons.

20 Friday

The BBC announces plans to start a **Third Programme** on May 8 next year.
■ Many of Britain's **building workers** are choosing to stay in uniform rather than come out now under the Class B demobilization scheme, which means that they will be drafted wherever the Ministry of Labour sends them.
■ The BMA wants the release of 5,000 doctors from the forces because if an epidemic develops this winter, civilian doctors will not be able to cope with it.

become the new British and Empire Heavyweight champion.
■ **Princess Elizabeth** takes her first flight with the King and Queen from Northolt to Ulster in a Transport Command Dakota.

18 Wednesday

The Food Ministry says they have no idea how to stop the **queues** caused by the shortage of goods and lack of staff in food shops.
■ **Marshal Stalin**, President Truman and Prime Minister Churchill, accompanied by Labour leader Clement Attlee, *right,* meet at **Potsdam,** outside Berlin, in a news black-out.
■ Seven Army mules now wear parachutists' wings to show they have been dropped by parachute.

21 Saturday

The government has given local government new powers to step up the building of houses and the requisition of empty property.
■ Girls in the WAAF are going to school for 72 hours to learn how to be good mothers when they are demobbed.
■ Mr van Acker, the Belgian prime minister, makes a slashing attack on King Leopold in the Belgian Senate.

22 Sunday

Groucho Marx, *right*, marries Catherine Marvin Gorcey, a 24-year-old singer. She was formerly the wife of Les Gorcey, one of the film *Dead End Kids*.

■ Film producer **Herbert Wilcox**, just back from the USA where he has arranged the distribution of his film *I Live In Grosvenor Square* throughout the USA, says America has never been more eager to see British films.

23 Monday

Allied **cruisers** sail into Tokyo Bay.

■ Because of the increase in **crime** in recent months, more policemen are to be demobbed. More than 15,000 recruits will be needed in the next two years.

■ The trial of **Marshal Pétain** (89) for high treason starts in the Paris law courts. 500 armed policemen will be on duty at all times.

24 Tuesday

The Ministry of Food say that Britain will take all surplus Canadian **eggs** until the end of 1947.

■ Because many **children** are absent from school for weeks at a time while their shoes are being repaired, the Welfare Education Committee has written to the Board of Trade to ask them to manufacture stronger shoes for children.

■ Men's **underwear** is in such short supply in Detroit, Michigan, USA, that men are buying women's undies for their own use.

25 Wednesday
Full moon

About 600 troops will unload **food** at Surrey Docks unless the dockers resume work.

■ Sensation at the **Pétain trial** when **Paul Reynard** is charged by Edouard Dalardier with having tried to make a secret deal with Mussolini behind Britain's back. Reynard denies it vigorously.

26 Thursday

US soldiers have decided that English girls are the **best kissers**, according to a survey carried out by *Stars and Stripes*, the US forces newspaper. English girls in their turn prefer the Americans when it comes to kissing. ■ Australian wives of US servicemen in Australia are to start a two-week course to prepare them for life in the States. The organizers of the course will tell them about social conditions, the type of clothes to wear, and how to cook the American way.

■ Golfer **Henry Cotton** is beaten by one of his assistants, Richard Knight, in the fourth round of the match play championship at Walton Heath.

27 Friday

The **General Election** result: **Labour** wins with 393 seats. The Conservatives retain 189 seats. The Liberals are almost totally wiped out. 24 women are elected— all Labour. Clement Attlee becomes Prime Minister (salary £10,000).

■ The US Army is in urgent need of **dogs** to sniff out Japanese soldiers hiding in trees

ATTLEE LEADS HIS LABOUR TEAM TO ELECTION LANDSLIDE

and caves; 800 are required by September 15. They want Belgian sheepdogs, Doberman Pinschers, Collies—anything with a good nose.
■ The UK, USA and China send an **ultimatum to Japan** to give in now or be wiped out.

28 Saturday

Attlee appoints six ministers: **Herbert Morrison**, Leader of the House (salary July 28, £5,000); **Ernest Bevin**, Foreign Secretary (salary £5,000); **Hugh Dalton**, *right*, Chancellor of the Exchequer (salary £5,000); **Stafford Cripps**, President of the Board of Trade (salary £5,000); **William Jowett**, Home Secretary (salary £5,000) and **Arthur Greenwood**, Lord Privy Seal (salary £5,000). Attlee flies to **Potsdam** today to continue the Big Three conversations, accompanied by Mr Bevin, the new foreign secretary. Although invited, Mr Churchill and Mr Eden are not returning.

29 Sunday

The *Domesday Book*, **Wellington**'s dispatches from Waterloo, the logs of the *Victory* and the *Bounty*, and other famous documents belonging to the Public Record Office, have returned to London. They had been stored for the duration of the war in a prison in Shepton Mallet, Somerset.
■ Yesterday a Mitchell **bomber crashed** into the 1,250 foot high **Empire State Building** in New York, completely wrecking the 78th and 79th floors, killing16 including three crew members, and injuring 26. Brilliant orange flames leaped as high as the 86th-floor observatory. The total damage is estimated at £125,000. Burning petrol cascaded down to the 76th and 75th floors. Luckily, as it was a Saturday, most of the offices were empty.

30 Monday

Mr Attlee says thank-you for the thousands of good luck messages that have been pouring into Downing Street from all over the world since the General Election.
■ Members of the **TGWU** are to urge the new Labour government to lower the voting age to 18.
■ Winston Churchill refuses the offer of the **Order of the Garter** and says he will remain plain mister.

31 Tuesday

Britain's **shipyards** swing into action as orders for new ships to replace those lost in the war steadily accumulate.
■ The **Potsdam** Conference draws to a close amidst feelings of mutual distrust between the Allies.
■ To show service people what a prefab is like, the War Office is sending three overseas —two for India and one for Burma—with ATS to act as demonstrators.

AUGUST

1 Wednesday

New parliament meets.
■ **Pierre Laval**, former French prime minister (1931-32 and 1934-36), virtual head of the Vichy government which collaborated with the Germans, and probably the most hated man in France, flies from Spain to Austria to **surrender** to the US occupation forces. They hand him over to the French Army.
■ Field Marshal Sir Harold Alexander becomes Governor-General of Canada.
■ Kayser Bondor promise that two pairs of fully-fashioned **stockings** in the latest hue are guaranteed to every woman on demob.

2 Thursday

Pierre Laval is back in Paris at Fresne Gaol.
■ **London Zoo** is expecting a baby elephant, a buffalo, two leopards, a lion andother animals from Kenya, the first for five years.
■ The **King** and **President Truman** will meet at Plymouth aboard the British battle cruiser *Renown*. After lunch the president will return to the *USS Augusta*, and the King will visit him later to take his leave.
■ **Princess Juliana** of the Netherlands and her three daughters, who have spent most of the war in Canada, leave Hendon on their way home to Holland.

ONE CREW . . .

The crew of the Boeing B-29 bomber, **Enola Gay** (above), her payload (below) and (right) the destruction wrought on one Japanese city on August 6 1945.

PLUS ONE BOMB . . .

EQUALS . . .

ARMAGEDDON at HIROSHIMA

3 Friday

The **Potsdam** Conference on the future of Germany decrees that all war plant is to be demolished and the Germans are not to be governed by a central government in Berlin, but by democratically elected provincial governments. On his return from Potsdam Mr Attlee issues the text of a message to **Winston Churchill** from the Big Three, thanking him for his work in the first part of the conference, and the untiring efforts and unconquerable spirit with which he served the common cause of victory and peace:

'The whole world knows his work and it will never be forgotten.

■ **Australia** will admit 50,000 orphans from Britain and Europe over the next three years, but adults will have to be regulated because of the shortage of housing and limited shipping to carry them to Australia.

■ **Alois Hitler**, half-brother of the Fuehrer, who owned a cafe in Berlin and has been hiding with false papers, has been **arrested** in the British Zone.

4 Saturday

The Queen's birthday

The Minister of Labour, **George Isaacs**, breaks the deadlock in the national rail talks. Negotiations will continue on Tuesday—but no trains will run tomorrow.

■ The **Civil Service** retains the marriage bar—only unmarried women and widows are eligible to take the Civil Service exams, the first to be held since 1939.

■ Alois Hitler is released by the British. A British military government statement says it is obvious that he has led a perfectly blameless existence, and was scared of being associated with the Fuehrer.

5 Sunday

Marshal Tito of Yugoslavia calls for a republican system of government.

■ Freak **storm** in Upper Weardale, Co. Durham. 2ins of snow falls between Edmondsbyers and Stanhope, followed by hailstones as big as marbles. Stratford-on-Avon is under 2ft of water.

6 Monday
Bank holiday

Reports from all parts of the country of packed seaside beaches. At some crowded resorts many slept overnight in deckchairs in the open. The roads are reported to be back to something like their pre-war appearance.
■ The US airforce Boeing B-29 Bomber **Enola Gay** drops the first atomic bomb on the Japanese city of **Hiroshima.**
■ A small shipment of champagne from France, the first since the liberation, is expected shortly.

7 Tuesday

H G Wells (79) in bed at his London flat, tells his staff that the A-bomb would wipe out everything, bad or good, in the world. It was not really news to Wells, though. He forecast it 12 years ago in *The Shape of Things to Come.*
■ Because more than 2,000 children die each year from TB caused by infected **milk**, doctors are again calling for compulsory pasteurization of all milk sold to the public.

8 Wednesday
New moon

Japanese radio is sending out **panic** calls to all its citizens to leave the cities threatened by the atomic bomb.
■ Notting Hill, London, had a bombing raid of sorts last night. The air was black with **birds**, as hundreds of starlings swooped down over buses and cars. Pedestrians ducked to avoid them.
■ **King Peter** of Yugoslavia withdraws the authority he gave to the regents.

9 Thursday

Fires are raging in **Hiroshima**. Unofficial estimates in Guam were that 100,000 people may have been killed or wounded. It is later disclosed that **60,000** were **killed** and 100,000 injured. Almost all houses in a nine-mile radius were destroyed. Allies drop an atomic bomb on **Nagasaki**. Panic-stricken Japan makes a move for **peace**.
■ **Russia** declares **war** on Japan. By 3pm units of the Red Army are striking at Japanese forces all along the Manchurian border.
■ Two French competitors, Henri Nele and Charles van Lerberghe, are accused of hitching a 60-mile lift in a lorry on the five-day Brighton to Glasgow cycling marathon.

10 Friday

The first import reports since 1938, published by the Board of Trade today, show that Britain has not imported a single **banana** since 1941. In the whole of 1944, Britain, with a population of 40 million, imported just 1lb of silk yarn, and one motor car worth £200. We also imported 922,907 watches and 3,796,916 false teeth.

11 Saturday

The Big Four —USA, UK, USSR and China—are consulting on the **Japanese surrender offer** which was officially sent to the Allies by Sweden and Switzerland.
■ **Pu-Yi**, the puppet emperor of Manchuria and one-time boy Emperor of China, will face trial as a quisling.
■ **Disney** announce their new production programme: *Make Mine Music* with Dinah Shore, Nelson Eddy and Benny Goodman (which they hope will do for swing music what *Fantasia* did for classical music), *Uncle Remus*, *Alice in Wonderland* and *Peter Pan.*

12 Sunday

An Australian sergeant, reluctant to leave his English girlfriend (5ft and blonde) behind when he was **repatriated**, packed her into an officer's valise and carried her aboard the liner at Liverpool. At Panama she was put ashore to await the first ship going to England.
■ Thousands of people lined the shores of Southampton Water yesterday as the *Queen Mary*, still in her warpaint but with all the guns removed, docked for the first time since

FINALLY, JAPAN SURRENDERS!

What began with the famous raid on Pearl Harbour in December 1940 finally ends with Japan's total, unconditional capitulation, following the unleashing of the Atom Bomb. Mountbatten, in Singapore, and (inset) Gen Douglas MacArthur with Japanese Foreign Minister Shigemitsu aboard the USS Missouri, accept the surrender

the eve of war, escorted by a swarm of small craft, bombers, fighters and trainer planes. Within 5mins, US soldiers and stevedores were loading the equipment and stores of the US 30th Division, sailing home next Friday.

13 Monday

Admiral Halsey's Third Fleet is steaming off Japan ready to sail into Tokyo Bay to receive the **Japanese surrender**.
■ The **grouse season** opens today because the 12th was a Sunday. Birds are very scarce—

about one tenth of the normal number.

14 Tuesday

Japan surrenders. The prime minister broadcasts at midnight from 10 Downing Street. Japan has accepted the Allied terms unconditionally, to spark more joyous scenes in London (left). Hundreds of civil servants will be rushed to Malaya, Siam, Hong Kong and other places in the Far East to take over their administration. Mr Attlee announces that the 15th and 16th will be VJ-Day holidays.

15 Wednesday
VJ Day (1)

Piccadilly is caught napping at midnight with only about 100 people around **Eros**. By 1.30am there are thousands. By 2am the march to Buckingham Palace begins, and great crowds pack into the Mall and Trafalgar Square. After the midnight broadcast, thousands of people set off from the suburbs in lorries, horse-drawn carts, on motorcycles and bicycles.

■ Great crowds of **weeping Japanese** gather before the Imperial Palace in Tokyo.

■ The opening of Parliament. The King's Escort of the Household Cavalry is dressed in khaki.

■ Sir Ben Smith, Food Minister, says that there is no prospect of any improvement in rations: fats and bacon - no hope of more; sugar—not to be cut below 1/4lb per week; dried eggs—less of them; shell eggs—more of them; tomatoes—more soon; dried milk —enough to make four pints each eight weeks this winter.

16 Thursday
VJ Day (2)

From one end of the country to the other, victory beacons blaze and people dance and sing. All over the country there are street parties *(right)*. The greatest crowd ever gathers before Buckingham Palace. The two princesses (aged 19 and 15) watch their parents on the balcony from the crowd. At 1.30am the crowd outside the palace lights a bonfire in the roadway, and stokes it with wooden park chairs. Mr Attlee, Mr Morrison and Mr Bevin appear on the balcony of the Ministry of Health.

17 Friday

The bells of **Westminster Abbey** are rung for three hours starting between 4pm and 5pm.

■ **Aneurin Bevan**, Minister of Health, is to run Britain's housing drive.

■ **General de Gaulle** commutes the death sentence on Marshal Pétain (89) to life imprisonment.

■ Motorists will be able to save up their basic **petrol allowance** from one month to another for holidays. New petrol ration gives cars up to 9hp—15 gallons for three months; 10-13hp—18 gallons; 14-19hp—24 gallons; 20hp and over 25 gallons for three months.

FASHION: Pencil-slim outlines are the news. Suits with narrow skirts, some of them so sheathed and tight-fitting that they will have side splits up to the knee to allow walking freedom. Alternatively, the skirts have a plain front and two small box pleats at the back. Jackets are longer—wrist length; street dresses are moulded to the figure, some with bustles and hip-draping peplums.

18 Saturday

Britain's **miners** are told that an extra eight million tons of coal will be needed this winter. The government is taking steps to get miners in the forces back to the pits.

■ **Football coupons** are going through the post again for the first time since the war started.

■ Within 24 hours of his appointment, Mr Bevan sends out instructions to all **housing** authorities in England and Wales for immediate action on permanent house construction.

19 Sunday

Thanksgiving service at St Paul's Cathedral.

"Here you are! Don't lose it again!"

PHILIP ZEC'S VIEW

"They got the victory—I hope they've got the moral . . ."

■ First reports appear in the newspapers about Radiolocation—**RADAR** for short—which came into existence four years before the war and immediately became the focus of work for hundreds of scientists. When the war came, a chain of stations round the British coast was in existence to give us warning of the approach of enemy raiders.

20 Monday

Surrender talks begin in Manila.
■ A railwayman who saved a town of 4,500 people has just received his reward from the railway company—one guinea. Mr Walter Ward (62), signalman of Brigg, Lincs, put out a fire in an ammunition train two weeks after VE Day, and prevented 500 tons of high explosive from blowing up the train and wrecking the town. The townspeople want to open a fund for Mr Ward to show their appreciation.
■ **Vidkun Quisling**, *right*, one-time Fuehrer of Norway, goes on

trial in Oslo for treason.
■ Reports from the US that **Lend-Lease** (the scheme by which the USA undertook to supply weapons and equipment to countries fighting Germany and its allies in return for the right to use certain Allied bases) will end, causes alarm in the UK and Europe.

21 Tuesday

Japanese war lords declare that it is necessary to maintain armed Japanese forces to keep law and order.
■ Battles are still raging along a 300-mile front **in Burma**. Lord Louis Mountbatten has radioed orders to the commander of the Japanese southern army to send an envoy to Rangoon on Thursday to arrange an orderly surrender.
■ Large stocks of women's winter coats may be sold without linings as manufacturers have nothing to line them with. The Board of Trade has given permission for half-lined coats to be sold, but now the trade wants permis-

sion to sell completely unlined coats.

■ A **Burmese jungle,** complete with dead Japanese in the undergrowth and the correct temperature, has been constructed for the Victory over Japan exhibition on a bomb site in Oxford Street, London.

■ VJ crowds celebrating in Inverness caused £1,000 worth of damage.

. . . The price of PETROL drops 2d. to 1s. 11 1/2d. a gallon. . .

22 Wednesday

Government launches a **survival plan** for the switch from war to peace. One less clothing coupon per person until next April, and less sugar for beer and confectionery, although the householder's rations will remain the same.

■ The US Congress has an odd problem on its hands—what to do with the £4,500 in royalties on the US sales of *Mein Kampf* by Adolf Hitler!

■ US army cooks in Okinawa bake a 600lb 32-layered **victory cake**. It has pink frosting and is topped by a sugar VJ. It feeds nearly 2,000 men, and contains 200 eggs; 150lbs sugar; 100lbs butter; 150lbs flour; 5 gals milk; 1lb salt; 1qt vanilla; 2lbs baking powder; 90lbs jam.

23 Thursday
Full moon

England wins the last **Victory Test** against Australia at Old Trafford by six wickets. It is the first time England has won there for 40 years.

■ Australian airmen in England, given indefinite leave and told to find jobs while their transport home is arranged, are still fighting but with a dif-

ference. About 400 of them have signed on as film extras and are Roman gladiators in *Caesar and Cleopatra,* filming at Denham Studios.

. . . STALIN announces the occupation of Manchuria.

24 Friday

Chandra Bhose, who would have been the quisling leader in India had the Japanese conquered the country, dies in a plane crash on his way to Tokyo. He had spent most of his 49 years in gaol.

■ More than 100 factory workers go berserk when film star **Michael Rennie,** *above,* pays a visit to their factory. They tear his coat, snatch off his tie, steal his handkerchief and nearly knock him out. He escapes to an office where he is given first aid.

■ Field Marshal **Montgomery** finds Rommel's magnificent Arab stallion, in Schleswig-Holstein.

25 Saturday

Lord Halifax, the UK ambassador to the USA, and Lord Keynes are on their way to Washington for discussions on the cancellation of Lend-Lease.

■ Dr Walter Hunziker, Director of the Swiss Tourist Federation, is in London negotiating an exchange scheme which may give British workers a week's **winter sports** holiday in Switzerland for £15.

■ **Pluto,** the Channel pipeline system, *left,* which fed a million gallons of petrol a day to the Western Front during the last months of the war, is being dismantled by British troops.

. . . PRESIDENT TRUMAN ratifies the UN Charter. . .

26 Sunday

The *Queen Elizabeth, right,* leaves Southampton with 15,000 US servicemen and airmen on board. The RAF central band plays on the quayside, as she is towed from the harbour, and two Meteors fly over in salute. Among the passengers on board is Col James Stewart, the film star.

■ Air Chief Marshal **'Bomber' Harris**, *left,* says he will retire in September.

27 Monday

Admiral Halsey's fleet will sail into **Tokyo Bay** today. It includes 12 of the world's biggest battleships, many mighty cruisers, and 100 destroyers.

■ Thousands of PoWs dance and cheer as planes drop food parcels into camps in Japan, Siam and China.

28 Tuesday

Thirteen transport planes touch down outside Tokyo with the first Allied landing party. **General MacArthur**, who will use Emperor Hirohito's palace at Sagami Bay as his HQ in Japan, left Manila last night. Chiefs of the SEAC led by Lt Gen Browning, meet the Japanese surrender envoys in the ballroom of Government House, Rangoon.

■ Women will find more give and stretch in super-quality **corsets,** says the secretary of the Corset Trade Association. Better supplies of rubber, steel and elastic will enable them to turn out improved utility ranges.

29 Wednesday

Rabbits, hares and goats from New Zealand will help eke out Britain's meat rations this winter.

■ Because engineers believe there is **oil** in the snow-encrusted land on the northwest tip of **Alaska** and the Arctic, an exploratory party of the US Navy is prospecting the area. Previously, only whaling ships and dog teams have penetrated these bleak zones.

30 Thursday

Black **grapes** at 2s. a lb (usually 30s.) or peaches and nectarines at 1d. each (3s. elsewhere), are available to the staff of E K Cole at their radar factory in Malmesbury, Wilts. When they bought the house, the hothouses were thrown in , and now the fruit is sold in the factory canteen to employees with sick relatives. So many appeared to have sick relatives they now need medical certificates.

■ Allied planes at the rate of 15 an hour for 24 hours a day will bring in the entire US 11th Airborne Division to **Tokyo**. The planes will be sent back carrying PoWs.

■ A British naval force enters **Hong Kong**. There is fierce hand-to-hand fighting as Japanese suicide snipers resist orders to surrender, and fight until killed or captured.

31 Friday

King Leopold of the Belgians has obtained permission to live in Switzerland providing, he doesn't go in for politics.

■ **Barbara Hutton**, the Woolworth heiress, and **Cary Grant,** *left,* are divorced.

■ US soldiers in Britain are advised to withdraw their money from British banks as the Treasury cannot guarantee holding the present exchange rate of $4.025 = £1.

SEPTEMBER

1 Saturday

The trial at **Nuremberg** of Goering, Hess and other top Nazis may be postponed again as the floor of the courthouse where they are to be tried has collapsed, probably because of bomb damage.

■ Press **censorship** ends at 9am today.

■ Two women grocers from Walworth, London, hire a coach and take the customers who stuck with them through the raids on a charabanc trip to the seaside. On the way to Southend they stop for a picnic—20 crates of free beer, ham, egg, and corned beef sandwiches, and a free packet of cigarettes for everyone.

2 Sunday

The **Japanese** sign the instrument of surrender aboard the **USS Missouri** in Tokyo Bay.

■ For £10 down and nine monthly instalments, farmers may buy a cow, and they don't need to pay cash. The payments can coincide with their monthly credits from the Milk Marketing Board—as they are paid they reduce the debt for their cows.

■ **Oranges** go on sale in Birmingham this weekend. 52,000 cases were landed at Southampton—too small a shipment for London and too large for smaller towns.

3 Monday

Russia is to present **Poland** with a fleet of 23 fully armed and equipped ships, including a destroyer, to form the nucleus of a Polish fleet in the Baltic.

■ The military **guards** on 10 Downing Street are removed.

4 Tuesday

The search for **Martin Bormann**, Hitler's deputy, who was last seen in Hamburg on May 11-12, spreads to internment camps in the British zone in Germany.

■ Mr Attlee warns of chaos if demob plans

YANKS GO HOME — WITH MORE THAN BAGGAGE!

An outstretched hand reaches over the side of a freighter at a British dockside—and a young woman, *right,* heads off for a new life in a new world thousand of miles from home. Other young British women, however, opted to do things more officially, by tying the knot before departing. . . .

are scrapped, but the speed of release will be doubled.

■ An advertisement in the *Tokio Shimbun* offers jobs to 500 waitresses, preferably with some English, for restaurants to be opened especially for the US occupation troops in Tokyo and Yokohama.

■ **DDT** is now available in small quantities for sale to the public.

■ The TUC asks the government to nationalize Britain's **transport** services immediately.

. . . Pre-war NAIL POLISH, which cost 3s.6d., is on sale on the black market for 15s. . .

much less wheat. We are, however, producing more sheep, pigs and poultry. Production has come to depend on PoWs, of whom 54,500 are working on the land this year against 25,300 last June.

■ Battle of the fleas in Dublin. Girls going to dances in Dublin are powdering themselves with flea powder, as **Dublin** is visited by a **plague of fleas**. Squads of men with sprayers are visiting hospitals, institutions and houses, smearing the walls and windows with insecticides, but the fleas seem to be winning.

■ British, Indian and Ghurka troops arrive in **Singapore** and, much to their surprise, are given a 'civic reception' by the Japanese commander.

6 Thursday

An American congressman says that **Bermuda** is of little use to Britain, and proposes the island should be ceded to the USA as a consideration of Lend-Lease aid.

■ More than 1,000 PoWs a day are being flown out of Bangkok, Siam.

■ German film stars and directors have been approached by **Hollywood** and British film studios, a senior British Army officer in German says.

■ An RAF **Mosquito** flies the Atlantic, east to west, in the record time of 7hrs 2 mins, knocking five hours off the best previous crossing.

7 Friday

4,000 infantrymen and 200 armoured crews of the Four Powers take part in the Allied **Victory parade** in the Tiergarten, Berlin. The salute is taken by Marshal Zhukov (USSR), General Patton (USA), Lt. General Sir B Robertson (GB), and General Koeltz (FR).

5 Wednesday

The **Morris 10**, *right,* goes on sale to those who have a permit to buy for £295 for the two-door fixed head model. The sliding-head saloon is £305, including five wheels and tyres, plus purchase tax of £82.13s.11d. and £85.9s.5d. respectively.

■ There are 25,300 fewer people working on the land this year than last, and we are growing fewer **potatoes** and

■ Fire watchers' **steel helmets** are on sale for 3d. Suggested uses; hanging flower baskets or chicken food receptacles.

■ There are estimated to be five million **surplus women** in Germany. During the last months of the war, Allied troops came across town after town populated almost entirely by women and old men.

8 Saturday
Jewish new year 5706

Train crash at Sunbank Halt, Llangollen, Wales, when the Shropshire Union Canal bursts its banks. On board is between £100,000-£200,000 due for delivery to post offices along the Welsh coast to pay Army allowances and old-age pensions. The fireman and guard both escape without injury.
■ US film **censors** demand changes in two British films, *Fanny by Gaslight* and *Henry V*, on moral grounds. They require a chaperone for **Phyllis Calvert** and **Stewart Granger** in *Fanny by Gaslight*, and they want no mention of the 'whore of Babylon', 'dastard 'and 'bastard' in *Henry V*.
■ **Undies** take on new colours this autumn, and gone will be the old hit-and-miss sizes of SW, W and OS. The customer will be able to buy by bust measurement, with two lengths for every size. There will be allowances for women with extra inches gained by starchy wartime diets, as well as specific in-between sizes.

STARS CENSORED!

Phyllis Calvert and Stewart Granger

9 Sunday

Japanese **General Okamamura** surrenders the million land, sea and air forces in China to the Chinese. The formal surrender of SE Asia and the Dutch East Indies will be made to **Lord Louis Mountbatten** in Singpore on Wednesday.
■ 200 artificial limbs made from bamboo—some with flexible joints—were made by doctors in a PoW camp at Nakhon Pathon in Siam. Over 700 operations were performed with homemade instruments, and 170 appendices removed without a single death.
■ The first **motor races** to be held in Paris in over six years took place today in the Bois de Boulogne.

10 Monday

Meat rationing is being reintroduced in Canada, where it was dropped in February 1944, to provide meat for the people of the liberated countries.
■ Old Age Pensioners are organising country-wide petition weeks to ask parliament for basic pensions of 30s. a week at the age of 60.
■ French **housewives wage war** against 'under the counter' shopkeepers in Paris. They march through Montmartre and stone the shops of butchers who had posted signs saying 'no meat this week'.
■ **Vidkun Quisling** is sentenced to death in Oslo, Norway.

11 Tuesday

A new drug called **Streptomycin**, discovered by two US scientists, may be used to combat many diseases, including TB, where penicillin has failed. It has had good results with whooping cough and some forms of meningitis.
■ A Johannesburg, S Africa, sweet manufacturer is sending 10 tons of **sweets** to Britain as a gift.
■ **Stalin** has approved the plans for a complete rebuilding of Stalingrad at a cost of £20 million.
■ The bill for **Blitz damage** in Britain so far is £271,181,171. 3,750,000 buildings are damaged, Nine out of 10 of them houses and shops.

12 Wednesday

A fly-free house could soon be yours. Paint containing DDT, the miracle **insect killer,** is now on sale in the shops. The paint retains its killing effect for a year or more, and costs 7s.3d. for 7lb. Guy's Hospital has received supplies. Reports indicate increased milk yield from fly-free cows where stables and cowsheds have been painted with whitewash containing DDT.

■ **General MacArthur** orders the arrest of the entire **Tojo** war cabinet (responsible for Pearl Harbor). Tojo, *right,* tries to commit hara kiri and is found unconscious. He is given a blood transfusion of American blood.

13 Thursday

Two million Londoners will get less **milk** this week. The ration is cut by half a pint to 2 pints.

■ **Lord Halifax**, head of the British Trade and Finance Mission to the USA, speaks about the difficulties facing Britain following the collapse of Japan and the stopping of **Lend-Lease** by the USA. He says that the British face a colder and hungrier winter than at any time during the war.

14 Friday

A **little black book** found in the Berlin headquarters of the Reich Security Police reveals the **Gestapo** list of seizures and arrests to be made as soon as the Wehrmacht landed in Britain. A special section names 35 publications whose offices were to be seized, the officers arrested and records confiscated. The list also includes the heads of exiled Allied governments, the administrators of universities, trades unions, the Co-op, the YMCA, the Society of Friends, Masonic Lodges, the Oddfellows and Rotary International, along with 389 other societies and 171 firms.

■ **General Peron**, Argentine Vice-President, Minister of Labour and dictator, calls upon the Army to resist all appeals to revolt when he reveals a new plot to overthrow the government.

15 Saturday

The **Duke of Windsor**, who abdicated from the British throne in 1936, left New York on Thursday, with the Duchess, for Le Havre. He tells reporters that he would like to set up a permanent home in England, and that he expects to visit England in the first or second week of October to see his mother for the first time in nine years.

■ Thanksgiving **Savings Week** opens in London, with an exhibitiion of war weapons. The most popular exhibit is the 49ft high V-2 rocket.

■ 300 fighter planes fly over London to commemorate the **Battle of Britain**, led by Group Captain Douglas Bader.

GARTH

BUILDING FOR THE FUTURE

The housing shortage is so acute that prefabs are the answer: *far right*; a large prefab estate in Great Yarmouth, *top right;* a prefab under construction, *bottom right*; a group of women curious to have a look at the inside, and *below,* a Nissen hut converted for residential use.

16 Sunday

Battle of Britain thanksgiving service at Westminster Abbey.

■ A jet-propelled **Vampire**, piloted by Captain Geoffrey de Havilland takes part in the flypast. It is Britain's fastest and most secret plane, and is said to have a speed of more than 500mph.

■ World-famous tenor, **Count John McCormack** (61), dies in Dublin. Born in Athlone, Ireland, in 1884, he was created a

count by Pope Pius XI in 1928.

17 Monday

William Joyce, Lord Haw Haw, goes on trial at No 1 court Old Bailey, charged with **high treason**. The Attorney General, Sir Hartley Shawcross, prosecuting, says Joyce is a British citizen, and the first witness produces a letter from Joyce's father, written in October 1922, which confirms it.

■ A 10,000 year-old place of habitation has

been discovered in Bromme, Denmark, and it supports the theory that Denmark was already inhabited when the climate was like today's Russian Arctic.

in the shops before the end of the present rationing period. They will have cotton tops, as this allows double the number of stockings to be produced.

18 Tuesday

Bristol Housing Committee decides to requisition every house in the city offered for sale with vacant possession to avoid houses only going to the rich.

■ Supplies of **nylon stockings** should be

19 Wednesday

Sir Ben Smith, Minister of Food, says **bananas** will be on sale in Britain early in the new year when the first cargo from Jamaica is due.

■ **Rubber** hot-water bottles will be on sale

soon. Sick people and expectant mums will get priority and should take a medical certificate to their shopkeeper. Prices will range from 7s.11d. to 12s.11d., including purchase tax.

20 Thursday

At No 1 Court, Old Bailey, **William Joyce** (Lord Haw Haw), is found **guilty** of high treason and sentenced to death.
■ Dr John Bond of Winnipeg, Ontario, Canada, who died in August, left £6,079 to the British government towards the cost of the war.
■ Crofters in the **Shetland Islands** have earned £3,000 in the past two years by getting rubber from the sea. It was washed up from wrecked ships, and the crofters get £2 for every bale as salvers award.

21 Friday
Full moon

An urn containing the heart of **Chopin**, Poland's greatest composer, which was hidden during the Occupation, has been returned to the Holy Cross Church, Warsaw.
■ Britain's **purchases** from the USA are being drastically cut pending the conclusion of a long term US-UK financial aid agreement. Until then all goods have to be bought for cash or for interest-bearing credit. Outstanding orders for prefabs, tobacco (during the war we bought £75 million-worth a year!) and cotton are cancelled.

22 Saturday

Dancer **Fred Astaire** (45), *left*, tells Hollywood that he is retiring from films. He says he and his doctors agree that he should have a rest.
■ The first supplies of **wallpaper** to be made since the war will reach the shops in November.

23 Sunday

The **smallest rose** in the world is on display at the National Rose Society's autumn display in the Royal Horticultural Halls,

HOW DAMP WAS MY VALLEY . . .

(The story of the village that sank with very little trace)

Left, Ladybower Reservoir, the largest man-made lake in the country. *Above,* only the spire of the church remains above the water. *Below,* the quiet village of Derwent before it was drowned.

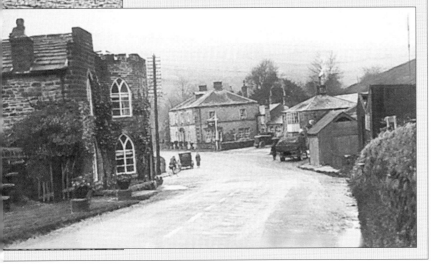

London. It is deep yellow and named Josephine Wheatcroft after the daughter of the grower, Harry Wheatcroft of Nottingham.

24 Monday

Mr Shinwell says that nationalization will be speeded up to help the fight to provide more coal.
■ All married women in the **WAAF** are offered their release. British soldiers serving in Germany are forbidden to marry German girls.

25 Tuesday

Java rises in bloodless revolution. **President Sukarno**, president by accla-mation, calls upon his followers to shed no drop of blood.
■ The UK has referred the question of the future of Palestine and Jewish immigration into the country to the United Nations.
■ The King and Queen open the Derwent Valley Water Board's **Ladybower** reservoir, the largest artificial lake in the country. Beneath it lies the village of **Derwent**. A number of **souvenirs** are buried, including a series of 1945 coins and a copy of *The Times* (see *main panel*).

26 Wednesday

New Zealand is sending Britain 30% more meat, 10% more butter, and 6% more cheese that has been released by stopping supplies to the US forces in the Pacific under reverse Lend-Lease.
■ Warner Brother's film *Objective Burma*, starring **Errol Flynn**, which shows the USA winning the war in Burma with the British and Australians nowhere, will be **withdrawn** from release. Criticism of the film has been vociferous in both Britain and the USA.
■ British ships sailing to Australia and New Zealand are going round by **Cape Horn**, an increase of 850 miles on the journey to New Zealand, to save the dollars needed to go through the Panama Canal.

■ Internationally acclaimed Hungarian composer, **Bela Bartok** (64), *left*, dies in the USA.

27 Thursday

Bevin Boys (those who worked down the mines instead of being conscripted into the Army) and others 'directed' to the pits, will be demobbed like soldiers in Class A—by age and length of service .

■ A **strike** by **lift operators** and building employees in New York brings the city to a standstill. 2022 buildings are affected. The government says the cost is £2 million per day. Tenants in affected buildings are refusing to pay rent if the owners do not reinstate services.

28 Friday

Children in many poor families in Britain this year will discover that **Father Christmas** has his HQ in Australia and New Zealand. People there are determined to see that Christmas 1945 is not an austerity one for British children. Melbourne already has hundreds of toys ready for posting and is planning thousands more. Christchurch, New Zealand, has adopted Manchester, and as well as toys is sending warm clothes for the under 5s.

29 Saturday

Mr Attlee has turned down suggestions that he should hold periodic **press** conferences like the US president. He feels that press conferences in the USA are very largely a substitution for parliament over here, and should be used sparingly and off the record to give background.

■ **Children** up to five years-old are going **barefoot** as the demand for their shoe sizes is four times greater than the number of shoes available. Retailers say their quotas disappear in minutes.

30 Sunday

The 8.20 Perth to London **express crashes** at Bourne End, Bucks, yesterday.

DEMOB COMES AT LAST

25 people are killed and more than 82 injured (*see panel page 79*).

■ The Mayoress of Hastings, Mrs Lancelot Blackman, has been **marooned** for 30 hours on board the sloop HMS Hastings. She only went for lunch. Hastings lifeboat has made two trips to try and get her off, but the seas were considered too high. Mrs Blackman will probably be disembarked at a naval port. She is reported to be well and comfortable.

OCTOBER

1 Monday

Ernest Bevin, the Foreign Secretary, has appointed a committee to look into the question of admitting women to the senior branches of the foreign service.

FOR THE BEVIN BOYS IN BRITAIN'S MINES

Because of the shortage of manpower in the coal mines, Ernest Bevin, Minister of Labout, announced in December 1943 that one in ten of the 18-25-year-old men called up would be ordered to work down the pits instead of going into the forces. These temporary miners became known as Bevin Boys.

King Leopold of the Belgians crosses into Switzerland to take up residence at Le Reposir, nr Geneva, where he will live with his wife, the Princess de Rethy, and his four children.

Tuesday

2 Sir Stafford Cripps, President of the Board of Trade, appoints Lt General Sir Wilfrid Lindsell—the man who organised the 8th Army's supply lines, and was quartermaster general for the BEF in September 1939 (he moved 158,000 men, 25,000 vehicles, and 40,000 tons of stores to France without a loss), to organise the gigantic factory switch from war to peacetime production.
■ A **kiwi**, the New Zealand symbol, a wingless bird that is both rare and shy, has been born for the first time in captivity in its native land. It took 80 days to hatch and the father did the hatching.

Wednesday

3 As 73,000 Post Office staff are still in the services, schoolboys and schoolgirls are being asked to help with the **Christmas mail** as they did last year. Those who volunteer to work between December 14-24 are promised relief from homework.
■ Bristol hospitals are putting **ice cream** on the patients' diet. The deputy medical officer of health says it is a first-class food, if the cream is there.

Thursday

4 **President Truman** sacks **General Patton** from the command of the US 3rd Army for keeping too many Nazis in top jobs.

He will take command of the 15th Army next Sunday.

■ France transmits two hours of **television**, the first since the outbreak of war. Programmes will be produced five days a week.

■ The Speyside **distilleries** have started producing malt whisky again.

■ The trial in Paris of **Pierre Laval**, virtual head of the Vichy government in France during the war, is suspended. The defence lawyers refuse to plead.

5 Friday

The **Duke of Windsor**, who abdicated from the British throne in 1936, arrives in Britain for a short stay with his mother, Queen Mary. The Duchess stays in France.

■ **Mr Bevin** suggests to his cabinet colleagues that they should visit Germany to see conditions for themselves.

■ Standard Cars announce that they are going to make Ferguson tractors, and employ 6,000 people in the aeroplane factory they have taken on from the government.

■ More drama at the trial of Pierre **Laval**. The defence lawyers appear, but Laval conducts his own case.

6 Saturday
New moon

The **RAF** has started to demob its aircraft. Some will be converted for civilian use, and others sold. The keenest buyers are expected to be flying clubs and civilian air schools whose planes were lost to the war effort. Also keen to buy are France, Holland, Belgium and Denmark.

■ The King, the Princess Royal and the Duke of Windsor dine with Queen Mary at Marlborough House.

■ There are **angry scenes** at the Laval trial in Paris between Laval, the judge and the jury, and the judge suspends the trial. Laval refuses to attend any more

sittings and his lawyers withdraw in protest.

7 Sunday

Chief prosecutors of the Four Powers in Berlin sign indictments of leading war criminals.

■ It is suggested by the Office of War Information that **Hollywood** should remove scenes showing lots of food from US films distributed abroad 'as it will cause nothing but ill will'.

8 Monday

Mr **Aneurin Bevan**, Minister of Health, has ordered local authorities to salvage steel, timber and bricks from ARP shelters, civil defence buildings, Anderson and Morrison shelters, and cleared military sites to provide materials for housing.

■ The Duke of Windsor accompanies Queen Mary on a **surprise visit** to London's East End. They drive in a closed car through some of the worst-bombed areas of Stepney, Poplar, Limehouse and the Isle of Dogs, but they are recognised and cheered.

■ **Ruldof Hess**, *left,* is flown from Madeley Airfield, nr Abergavenny, to Frankfurt, for trial at Nuremberg.

9 Tuesday

Coston is the new name for Ted Pappaconstantidimitriacoupoulous of Three Rivers, Michigan, USA. He found his original name rather cumbersome.

■ **Road accidents** in August were higher than they were last year when blackout was in force.

■ Pierre Laval is found **guilty** in his absence from court in Paris, and sentenced to death for treason.

10 Wednesday

The Argentine Ministry of the Interior announce that the dictator **Juan**

Peron, *left*, has resigned all his posts in the Government and is said to be under arrest. After the announcement, angry crowds gather outside government house, but it is believed that Peron has already fled the country.
■ A policeman discovers a **lion** and 16 **monkeys** on his beat. They had come from Ricco's circus which was travelling from Earby, Yorks, to Doncaster.

11 Thursday

The London and Liverpool **docks** grind to a standstill. Over 40,000 men are on **strike** and 300 ships are lying idle at the docks. Troops start to unload cheese and frozen fish at Hull. Minister of Labour, George Isaacs, says that the strike is unjustified. The Southampton dockers vote not to strike.
■ **GI brides** put on a massive demonstration at Caxton Hall, demanding the speed-up of their passages to the USA.
. . . It is the WARMEST October day in Falmouth, Cornwall, since records began in 1870. . .

12 Friday

Planes dropping **seed** from the air are helping to carry out a 500 million tree re-afforestation programme in Russia.
■ Preparations to double the size of **newspapers** have had to be abandoned because of Britain's shortage of foreign currency.
■ Britain is to get 260 million lbs of **meat** from the USA—one month's ration for the whole country.
■ General **Juan Peron** of Argentina is **arrested** by the Army.
. . .The temperature at Combe Martin, Devon, is 74°F.

13 Saturday

150 Labour MPs have signed a motion asking

ADVERTISERS' ANNOUNCEMENTS

war
or no war
you must look your best

for 18 years corot has been making it easy to obtain lovely frocks suits, coats, lingerie, etc., at modest prices on their easy payment plan.

why don't you call at our showrooms or order by post

price £12.2.2

making up price 8 gns.

ref. m 107

corot
33 old bond st., london, w.1

please send spring catalogue and full details
I enclose 2½d.

name
m.107 ....
address ....

the government to increase the **old age pension** by 7s.6d. for a single person and 12s.6d. for a married couple.
■ Dock leaders blame the **Communist** Party for the spread of the unofficial dock-strike. 43,000 of Britain's 75,000 dockers are now out, and the strike brings exports to a standstill.
■ London and the south east are so short of **salt** that the Ministry of Food is sending in extra supplies for the next two months.
■ **Haifa**, Palestine, will be the Mediterranean exit for the 1,000-mile-long 26in pipeline from Saudi Arabia to open up a vast new oil supply for Europe.
. . .The INDIAN SUMMER continues. There have now been 14 days without rain.

14 Sunday

Farmworkers in Normanby-le-Wold are threatening to quit unless water is brought to the village. They still depend on wells, and during the last few days the wells have run dry.
■ A couple living in Plymouth's first **prefab** complain that thousands of people have come to see what it is like. On the first day they were crowding all round the house and staring in through the windows.

15 Monday

Women, many ex-civil defence workers, are offering to help unload the food ships held up in the docks by the strike. 6,350 troops are at work on food ships today.
■ Pierre **Laval** is **executed** by firing squad at Fort Chatillon, Paris, after attempting suicide by taking poison.

16 Tuesday

The Ministry of War Tansport says that the arrangements for getting British servicemen

ACTION! THE MOVIES AND THE

The Top Films of 1945

HENRY V
ROAD TO UTOPIA
DILLINGER
MEET ME IN ST LOUIS
PICTURE OF DORIAN GREY
NATIONAL VELVET
SON OF LASSIE
MADONNA OF THE SEVEN MOONS
CAN'T HELP SINGING
A TREE GROWS IN BROOKLYN
STATE FAIR
THE SEVENTH VEIL
THE WAY TO THE STARS
A SONG TO REMEMBER
WILSON
NONE BUT THE LONELY HEART
BLITHE SPIRIT
A BELL FOR ADANO
THE LOST WEEKEND
FAREWELL MY LOVELY
TARZAN AND THE AMAZON
THE CONSTANT NYMPH
WESTERN APPROACHES
ARSENIC AND OLD LACE
TO HAVE AND TO HAVE NOT
THE KEYS OF THE KINGDOM
THE WICKED LADY
BRIEF ENCOUNTER
CAESAR AND CLEOPATRA
GOING MY WAY
FANNY BY GASLIGHT
THE RAKES PROGRESS

STARS OF THE SILVER SCREEN

Far left: Celia Johnson and Trevor Howard in *Brief Encounter*; left, Elizabeth Taylor and Mickey Rooney in *National Velvet*; and, below, Vivien Leigh and Claude Rains in *Caesar and Cleopatra*.

It's a wonderful year for British films which, at the end of the year, dominate the West End cinemas. Below, left to right, Bob Hope, Gary Cooper, Greer Garson, James Mason, Margaret O'Brien, Patricia Roc, Jean Simmons with Van Johnson, and Robert Donat.

RUGGLES

home will not be upset to speed the Atlantic crossing of GI brides.
- **Prefab** prices soar from £60 to £130.
- Four **cats** from a farm in Boston have been flown by bomber to Berlin to fight the mice that have overrun the capital.
- The Lord Mayor of Melbourne has opened a **Christmas appeal** for £100,000 to buy food for Britain.

17 Wednesday

Only 4,152 out of 165,000 prefabs have been built in the country so far, and the bill for construction has leapt from £150 million to £184,699,470.
- The **fats ration** is raised to 2ozs a week.
- **New £5 banknotes** are to be issued by the Bank of England because of the number of forgeries in Germany during the war.

18 Thursday

Mr Bevan hopes the **housing shortage** will have ended in four years. He appeals to householders to open up their homes to those in need. Local authorities will make adaptations where householders allow so that extra cookers and sinks can be provided.
- The pre-war luxury liner *Andes*, carrying Australian airmen home, covers the 12,000 miles from Liverpool to Melbourne in 23 days

6hrs, breaking the *Mauretania's* record of 28 days.
- **Coup in Argentina**. General Peron overthrows the government and sets up his own, but he remains out of office, and resigns from the Army.

19 Friday

The Ministry of Fuel and Power will control the cost of **logs**, because £20 a ton is being charged in big towns.
- The government announces that some wartime **airfields** are to be used for peacetime flying—Northolt, Heathrow and Prestwick. Gas turbine-propelled planes may soon be in civil service, but at present they are too uneconomic.
- Reuter reports that General **Peron** has gone to Patagonia for a rest

20 Saturday

The **Ministry of National Insurance** asks for an all-round increase of 5s. in minimum pensions payable to unemployed injured workmen. The present scale is 60s. per week for a single person, 76s. per week for a married person, and 83s.6d. per week for a married person with one child.
- Every householder in France must declare the number of **rooms** and members of the household. Two rooms will be allowed the

first two people, plus one room for each extra person. Bonuses will be offered to people leaving heavily populated cities other than Paris of £140 to an unmarried person, £300 for a family of two, and £30 for each extra person.

21 Sunday
Full moon

Two giant pandas for London Zoo are being hunted in China.
■ Scented **toothpicks** to appeal to women diners are the coming thing in the USA. Dentists would like toothpicks to become as socially acceptable in the USA as they are in Europe.

22 Monday

A man who arrived in Bristol last week to take a job went along to register for a house. He's 14,999th on the list. Bristol lost 4,000 houses in the Blitz.
■ The National Maritime Museum, Greenwich, reopens today.
■ Two white **cats** were taken in a hamper by lorry from their home in Beech, nr Alton, to Andover, 26 miles away. Two hours later one of them was back at its old home.

23 Tuesday

France swings to the **left**. The three left-wing parties have won more than a 4-1 **majority** in the election of the new Constituent Assembly.
■ An RAF Coastal Command **Mosquito** sets a new Atlantic record crossing from Gander, Labrador, to St Mawgan, Cornwall, in 5hrs 10mins. The previous record was 5hrs 39.5mins.

24 Wednesday

Income **tax cut** to 9s. in the £. Personal allowances for a single person are raised from £80 to £110; and from £140 to £180 for married couples. The exemption limit is raised from £110 to £120. If you are married with four children, you can earn up to £8.2s. a week and be tax free.
■ **Vidkun Quisling**, the Fuehrer of Norway, is **executed** for high treason.
■ The United Nations Organisation is formally called into being, 29 ratifications having been received.

24 Thursday

Coastal towns in southern England and Wales battered by a great gale. The sea defences are breached in 10 places and the estimated damage is £50,000.
■ From today you can buy five new utility handkerchiefs for 9s.9d. cotton and £1.2s. 6d. linen. The cotton handkerchiefs are made from surplus anti-gas cloth and balloon fabrics.
■ Film star **Ann Todd,** *left,* signs the biggest contract ever given to a British actress following her success in *The Seventh Veil*. She will be paid £200,000 for six films for Fox and eight films for Rank.

. . . No hope yet of whiter bread. The NATIONAL LOAF is to stay. . .

26 Friday

The number of **horses** receiving rations in England is 93,650; Scotland 12,076; Wales 8,254, apart from the 9,213 owned by the four main railway companies, who get separate rations.
■ To ease the shortage of **brassieres**, the Board of Trade may earmark the parachute fabric that was used to drop supplies, but even that is in short supply.

27 Saturday

The question of whether nose or paw should decide the winner of **greyhound** races has been settled in favour of the paw, say stewards of the Greyhound Racing Club.
■ The dock strike spreads to Northern Ireland.

■ 100,000 x-ray plates, 10ins x 12ins, found in the British zone in Germany, are being used to replace broken windows in damaged houses.

28 Sunday

Fighting breaks out in 11 Chinese provinces between the Chungking government and Communist forces, affecting more than 40 million people in northern China.
■ It is announced that **Sotheby's** will sell, on November 27, one of the most astonishing letters penned by a queen. It is the note that Queen Elizabeth wrote in 1572 to Charles IX of France on the possible marriage between herself and his younger brother, the Duc d'Alençon, then a youth of 20. The queen was 39 at the time.

29 Monday

The **Coronation Scot train**, which went to America's World Fair in 1939, is still there. The engine came back, but there was no space for the coaches, which were used to house US army officers. They will remain in the USA. New carriages will be built with **telephones** in the first-class carriages with a direct line to the buffet.
... Some DOCKERS return to work...

30 Tuesday

Mr Attlee is going to the USA on November 11, to discuss international affairs and share information on the **atomic bomb** with President Truman.
■ Britain is setting up an Atomic Energy Experimental Station at Harwell Airfield, nr Didcot, Berks, to carry out experiments into all uses of atomic energy.
■ A small quantity of date-and-treacle **puddings** in tins will soon be on the market.

31 Wednesday

28,000 troops to be drafted into the docks.
■ A US Army film, *Appointment Tokyo*, opens in the USA. The columnist in the *Hollywood Reporter* says that the film largely ignores the fact that UK, Australian, New Zealand, Dutch, Russian and US marines did

AS IF THE WAR WER

much of the fighting. No date for the release of the film in Britain has been announced.
■ **Vickers Armstrong** have orders for six ships as well as a new 29,000-ton liner for P & O.

Not Disaster Enough . . .

An empty train headed for Newhaven on September 2 to pick up servicemen coming home on leave, crashes into a railway tunnel just outside Haywards Heath. The driver and fireman are killed instantly. The Perth-Euston express that crashes at Bourne End on September 30 kills 25 and injures 82.

NOVEMBER

1 Thursday

Scientists at **Pye Radio** in Cambridge have discovered how to send both sound and vision on the same wave-length. This can be picked up and reproduced from one receiver and doesn't need, as now, two different sets. Televisions could be on the market soon for £40.
■ One of the air-speed-record-attacking

Meteors covers the Herne Bay course at 609mph.

2 Friday

British civil aviation is to be nationalized.
■ Dockers all over the country vote to return to work on Monday.
■ Children at a village school in Yorkshire are getting **telephone classes**. They are taught to make emergency calls, inquire about train times, book theatre tickets and

order goods for delivery by the grocer. No child will leave without these skills.

Saturday

3

Queen Wilhelmina of the Netherlands yesterday presented **Winston Churchill** with a beautiful Dutch 17th century tortoiseshell-work cabinet from the Rijksmuseum, in Amsterdam, containing 650 letters written by his ancestor, the 1st Duke of Marlborough to Hensius, then Chief Minister of Holland. The gift is a token of gratitude from the Dutch people.

Sunday

4

New moon

The 35-person strong **Moscow Dynamo** football team, including a radio commentator, three cameramen and a lady interpreter, arrived in Croydon last night. It is the first visit of a Russian football team to this country. They will stay 2-3 weeks and train at **Chelsea**. They needed an extra motorcoach for the several cwts of food they brought with them. Pictured above, action from their match against Chelsea at Stamford Bridge

Monday

5

US Army scientists, who have been studying **Mussolini's brain**, have so far found nothing to explain his actions.

■ Forty **nurses** on the night shift at St Bartholomew's Hospital, London, stage a lie-in-bed **protest** at the quality of food available for night staff. They say the day staff's food is much better.

Tuesday

6

Professional **footballers** threaten to **strike** on November 17, unless the Football

ANY VANTAGE POINT WILL DO FO[R]

NO RE-ADMISSION
BOVRIL BOVRIL
OXO [1/6] ADMIS

League meets their demands for an increase in wages.

■ 1lb tinned **puddings** for four points each and costing 1s. will be on sale in the next ration period, though there may not be enough to give one to each family.

Wednesday

7

28 million 1/4 lb tins of sardines are on their way from Spain.

■ The **Dagenham Girl Pipers** have been sent to Berlin to entertain the troops, but it is the Germans who are getting the biggest kick out of the unusual music.

■ Group Captain H J Wilson captures the **world air speed record** in a Meteor, with a speed of 606mph.

Thursday

8

William (Lord Haw Haw) Joyce's **appeal** is **dismissed**. His legal advisers will now appeal to the House of Lords.

■ **Tommy Lawton** joins Chelsea Football Club from Everton for £14,000—an all-time

E BIG MATCH . . .

The hottest ticket in town—that's Moscow Dynamo's soccer stars. Spectators will do anything to catch sight of the game at Chelsea (left and above). They saw more than the Dynamo goalkeeper (right) when the Russians played Arsenal in the fog on November 21

record transfer fee.

9 Friday

The **Lord Mayor's Show**. This year, for the first time, all the five regiments privileged to march through the City of London take part, as well as an ATS band.

■ 151,906 **Italian PoWs** presently in this country will be repatriated as soon as the beet and potato harvest are completed.

■ Three girls who put on **slacks** to serve in a grocery store in Trowbridge, Wilts, are sacked when they refuse to change into skirts.

10 Saturday

France's claim against Germany, submitted to the Inter-Allied **Reparations** Conference, which opened in Paris yesterday, is £25,845 million—£625 for every man, woman and child in France.

■ US planemakers **Lockheed** say they are making much better planes

than the Gloster Meteor, but they don't intend to make an attempt on the British record. They say their Shooting Star goes so fast they don't know how fast it can go, but they are sure it will beat the Meteor!

11 Sunday

Dominion Day, New Zealand

Jerome Kern (60), the composer of Show Boat, dies in New York.

■ **Remembrance Day**. Princess Elizabeth (19), in her ATS uniform, joins her father in laying a wreath at the Cenotaph, the first service there for seven years.

■ Radio Luxembourg has been returned by the Allies to the Luxembourg government.

12 Monday

Princess Elizabeth and **Princes Margaret** (15), accompanied by two officers of the Household Cavalry and the lady-in-waiting to

Princess Elizabeth, sit in the fourth row of the stalls at the Globe Theatre to see *While the Sun Shines*. It is their first visit to the theatre without the King and Queen.
■ The restriction regulating the length of men's **socks** is being withdrawn, but the coupon value will remain the same—two coupons per pair.

13 Tuesday

Professional **footballers** win £1 a week **pay rise** bringing the maximum wage to £9 per week. December 1 will also see the resumption of match bonuses—£2 for a win; £1 for a draw. On the field, **Chelsea** play **Dynamo Moscow** at Stamford Bridge. 85,000 people, of whom 74,496 paid for admission, fight for a view of the game from any vantage point, including the top of the stands. The Russian team appears with bouquets of red and white carnations for their opposite numbers. The result is a draw, 3-3. (See panel, previous page).
■ The Irish Government announces that visitors from N Ireland and Britain may bring motor cars with them, but they cannot be supplied with petrol in Eire.

14 Wednesday

Readers of Toronto's *Evening Telegram* have sent £5,500 to the Lord Mayor of London to provide children's **Christmas parties** in 11 poor and bombed London boroughs.
■ Mr Churchill has had to send back to the USA the **luxury plane** given to him by President Roosevelt last year. He cannot afford the repairs, and as he is no longer Prime Minister the money cannot be paid out of public funds.
■ There will be extra sugar, sweets, butter, margarine, meat and cheese as a Christmas bonus.
... CUP FINAL TICKETS will cost more next year— 2gns, 1gn, 10s. 6d. and 3s.6d. standing ...

15 Thursday

British **troops** fire on Jewish rioters in Tel Aviv, following Mr Bevin's suggestion of an Anglo-US enquiry to examine the problem of

NUREMBERG WAR TRIAL

Once, they ruled Europe and dined in style in her capital cities. Now, in captivity, they feast on meagre rations and face their accusers: Top, Doenitz, Jodl; above, Schacht, von Papen; right, Goering, Hess and other top Nazis.

Palestine and European Jewry, and the British government's refusal to increase the number of Jewish immigrants into **Palestine**.
■ For the first time in the history of cinema, **British films** will predominate in the West End of London with the release of *I Know Where I'm Going* and *The Wicked Lady*, followed by *Brief Encounter, Pink String and Sealing Wax* and *The Rake's Progress*. The showpiece will be *Caesar and Cleopatra*. British films also doing well in the USA are *Madonna of the Seven Moons* and *The Seventh Veil*.

16 Friday

Reinforcements of the 6th Airborne

EGIN . . .

president of France because the Communists demand one of the three main Cabinet posts before agreeing to become part of the government.

■ **Dynamo Moscow** football team plays Cardiff City at Ninian Park and beats them 10 -1.

18 Sunday

Dr W N Leek of Winsford, Cheshire, says that the wrong clothing may be responsible for the falling birthrate, citing the adoption of pyjamas instead of nightshirts coinciding with the diminishing birth-rate.

■ 90 **German scientists** are going voluntarily to the USA to work on atomic energy and rockets. Though not regarded as PoWs, they will be kept in custody, but will receive a modest salary.

19 Monday
Full moon

The remains of the beautiful Cayetana, **Duchess of Alba**, immortalized by the 19th century painter Francisco Goya, have been exhumed for historical investigation. The present Duke of Alba was at the ceremony.

■ The French parliament decides by 400 to 164, to **reinstate General de Gaulle**, provided he includes equal numbers from the three main parties (Communist, Socialist, and Popular Reform) in the government, and puts into force the Resistance Movement's programme of reform and reconstruction.

20 Tuesday

Prefab **aluminium houses** are being produced by five factories that formerly built bombers.

■ 24 top **Nazis** among whom are **Hess, Ribbentrop, Goering, Keitel, Streicher, Doenitz**, and **von Papen**, go on trial in Nuremberg. They face an indictment, separately and together, which is the most damning and comprehensive in the history of justice. (See panel, above).

... Dense FOG in the Channel...

Division are rushed to Tel Aviv.

■ The USSR is informed that Britain, Canada and the USA intend to keep the methods of manufacturing the **atomic bomb** a secret to maintain security, and recommend the setting-up of a United Nations organization to promote the use of atomic energy for industrial and humanitarian purposes.

17 Saturday

The government decides to give an additional £75 million to UNRRA so that its relief work in Europe can continue. The US government approves an additional £325 million for UNRRA.

■ **General de Gaulle resigns** as interim

HELLO . . .

The end of the Second World War
The United Nations
Gloster Meteor Jets
Prefabs
DDT
Family Allowances Bill
Mepacrine—substitute quinine
12 Black-footed Cape Penguins for London Zoo
Ice cream (again)
Women voting in France for the first time
Sunderland Flying Boat
The correct position of the Magnetic North Pole
Quick frozen fish
Photo finishes on racecourses
Juke boxes
Queues for everything
Britain's second Labour government
Atom bombs
Radar
Streptomycin
The Vampire aeroplane
Harwell Atomic Energy Experimental Station
Moscow Dynamo Football Team
The resurgence of the British film industry
PVC
The new Waterloo Bridge
Hagannah (Jewish Defence Force)
International Monetary Fund

Greetings: (from top), the end of the war in Europe; Waterloo Bridge, The A-Bomb, Clement Attlee's Labour success; and the Vampire jet.

GOODBYE . . .

No longer with us: (above) Bela Bartok, the composer, and Anne Frank, the young Dutch diarist; below, Franklin D Roosevelt, US President, Count John McCormack, and the Halifax bomber.

Tojo
Doodlebugs
Blackout
Wellington bomber
Agnes Baden Powell
Halifax bomber
The coalition, and finally caretaker, government
Lend-Lease
President Franklin D Roosevelt
Old Waterloo Bridge
Maurice Utrillo
Fernand Leger
Thomas Mann
Bela Bartok
Anne Frank
Dr Cosmo Lang — Archbishop of Canterbury
Pluto (the Channel pipeline system)
Martin Bormann, Hitler's deputy (last seen, Hamburg May 1945)
SW, W and OS sizes for women's clothes
General George (Blood and Guts) S Patton
Count John McCormack

. . . AND AUF WIEDERSEHEN . . .

. . . to Adolf Hitler, Josef Goebbels and Heinrich Himmler. . . .

. . . oh, and it's Ciao to Mussolini, too . . .

21 Wednesday

The RAF is hunting for a **stolen Meteor** jet, which disappeared from the RAF station at Molesworth, Hunts. It carried fuel for only 400 miles, and must have landed less than an hour from the airfield.
■ The Dynamo Moscow football team plays Arsenal. They face a team which includes only four or five Arsenal players. Arsenal say that as 44 of their 48 professionals are still in the services, they have recruited players from Spurs, Fulham, Bury, Stoke, Blackpool and Cardiff. Arsenal lose 3-4 in a fog so thick it is doubtful if any of the 5,400 spectators see anything.
■ **Robert Benchley** (56), author, actor, critic and humorist, dies in New York.

22 Thursday

Fog continues
■ The Communists fill five places in de Gaulle's cabinet.
■ The flag flown by the foremost British ship against the Spanish Armada in 1588 is presented to the US aircraft carrier *Enterprise* by the First Lord of the Admiralty at Southampton. The Japanese claimed to have sunk the Enterprise six times, after which she became known as the 'Galloping Ghost'.
■ **Princess Margaret** (15) has her appendix removed.

When she's back—

to the meals that mother makes.

ah! **BISTO**

FOR DELICIOUS GRAVY

23 Friday

A new substance—PVC—light, waterproof and hardwearing, makes its appearance as the plastic uppers on shoes. Backed with fabric, it looks like calf leather and was first used for miners' boots.
■ Because of the shortage of gamekeepers, **wildlife** in the Scottish Highlands is on the increase. A wildcat 34ins long has been caught at Inverlochy Castle, Inverness, and eagles are killing lambs and wild rabbits.
■ The Dynamo Moscow football team visits the racing-cycle works of **Claude Butler**, and accepts a gift of 11 bicycles. The Trade Delegation orders a trial assortment of 100 bikes for sale in Russian shop.
■ No more rationing in the USA except for sugar, of which there is a worldwide shortage.
■ **Charles Coborn** (93), the oldest working comedian in the world and best known for his two songs *Two Lovely Black Eyes* and *The Man who Broke the Bank at Monte Carlo*, dies in London.

24 Saturday

Clothing from stocks held by the WVS (both old and new) will be distributed to Assistance Board Depots throughout Britain to help clothe people who need it this winter. A small stock will be kept in reserve for any emergency.
■ The shortage of **teachers** is so great that five-year-olds cannot go to school as there is no one to teach them.
■ Because the RAF's petrol-burning device for dispersing fog, **FIDO**, is so expensive, the Ministry of Civil Aviation is planning experiments to control civil aircraft landings by instruments. FIDO will still be used on airforce fields.

25 Sunday

American Express announces holiday plans for US citizens if space on airliners allows. A two-week holiday in Europe will cost £212, and a three-week holiday £262.
■ The people of Scotland present **General**

Eisenhower with a flat for life at Culzean Castle, Ayrshire, with 2,000 acres of shooting at his disposal.

26 Monday

Jewish terrorists blow up two police coastguard stations north of Tel Aviv.
■ A French officer who offered the Germans two schemes to force Britain to her knees (1, dig a tunnel under the Channel and 2, blow up Gibraltar) has been brought before a French Military Tribunal.
■ Sold at **Sotheby's** for £3,400—the first illustrated edition of Boccaccio's *Decameron*, published in 1492.

27 Tuesday

Two elderly women, both dressmakers, from Lavender Hill, London, win the £1,000 prize at the Hammersmith Palais, London for composing the best new dance tune, *Cruising down the River*.
■ A letter from **Mary Queen of Scots** when she was captive in Fotheringay Castle, Northants, in 1587, is sold for £1,100 at Sotheby's. It will go to Scotland. Queen Elizabeth's letter (see October 28) fetched only £600.

28 Wednesday

Frinton, 'the most exclusive **seaside** town in Britain', has lost its only means of transport, a horse-drawn bus. The driver has retired and there is no one else to carry on. The townsfolk say they would rather walk than have motorbuses which, they think, would encourage trippers.
■ Dynamo Moscow football club play **Rangers** at Ibrox Park, Glasgow. It ends in a draw. A missed penalty by Rangers saved Dynamo from defeat.

■ From December 10, the beef sausage will have 2 1/2% more meat in it.
■ Fim star **Deborah Kerr** (22), marries Squadron Leader Anthony Bartley DFC (26), at St George's, Hanover Square, *above*.

29 Thursday

John Amery, *right*, ex-public schoolboy, West End playboy, son of a former Cabinet minister, and accused of high treason for his wartime broadcasts, changes his plea to guilty to save his family further distress, and is sentenced to death in a trial that lasts eight minutes. His younger brother, Captain Julian Amery, is the only member of his family in court.
■ Of the 9,000 British

brides of Canadian servicemen who have gone to Canada in the last three years, only 29 have applied to the Army to return to Britain.

■ The **Duke of Argyll** has finally agreed to sell his reservoir at Crosshill, Argyll to Campbeltown Town Council for £17,000 after 100 years of wrangling over water.

30 Friday
St. Andrew's Day

King Peter of Yugoslavia, *right,* is **deposed** and his country is now the Democratic Federal Peoples' Republic. The king and his family are deprived of all rights.

■ Mannequin Pat Niland, who wore a French-type swimsuit (brief trunks, brief bra) to a speedway meeting in Sydney, Australia, has been fined 10s. for offensive behaviour.

■ **Winston Churchill** celebrates his 71st birthday with a birthday cake in the shape of England.

DECEMBER

1 Saturday

The government of **Southern Rhodesia** proposes a scheme to the British government to train British ex-servicemen as farmers and settle them on their own land. They will initially take 100 men—60 of them bachelors (to give Rhodesian girls a chance).

■ Mr Shinwell says he hopes to avoid serious **coal shortages** this winter. Although the production of coal is better, it isn't as good as he had hoped.

2 Sunday

The prototype of the **Handley Page Hermes**, the biggest ultra-modern type of civil aircraft to be built in Britain, **crashes** five minutes after take-off at Colney St, nr St Albans, on its first test flight. Two people

were killed.

■ Twenty-four US and two Canadian cities fight to be the home of the UN headquarters. among them Atlantic City, Black Hills, South Dakota (which offers 100 square miles which could be internationalized), and Boston. Britain and France propose that the UN HQ should be in Europe.

■ Tenby, Wales, has 1/2ins of **rain,** and as much rain fell on London today as during the whole of November. Temperature 50°F.

3 Monday

Speyside **whisky** distillers have orders from all over the world that they have no chance of filling. They are only allowed 47% of the 1938 quota of grain for the manufacture of whisky. Publicans and black-market dealers in the south are offering wholesalers any price they like to ask.

■ FOR SALE: The government is selling off millions of pounds-worth of bedding, crockery, towels, cutlery, furniture and pots and pans—just part of the war assets being cleared from government dumps. Enough munitions and weapons to have waged war on Japan for another 18 months are also for sale.

4 Tuesday
New moon

Australia offers more food to Britain—30 million dozen eggs, 900,000 lbs egg powder; 12 million lbs egg pulp; 1million cases canned fruit, and 17,000 tons of meat. They also hope to step up shipments of butter, cheese, fresh fruit and jam.

■ Lt Commander E M Brown of the RNVR makes the first successful **landing** of a jet-propelled aircraft on the flight deck of the aircraft carrier *HMS Ocean.*

■ Twenty-five acres of glass is being used to re-glaze the roof of **Paddington** station. **The first fall of snow this winter—3ins in Buxton, Derbyshire.**

5 Wednesday

From today **licences** will no longer be needed to buy and sell secondhand or recon-

BELINDA

ditioned typewriters and office equipment.

■ Thousands of **monster rats** living along the river bank between Norwich and the Broads are in fact coypus, the 'fur coat' rats. A London firm is paying up to £5 for each pelt.

■ The **Dynamo Moscow** football team goes home after a party at the Russian embassy where they drink weak warm beer and eat spam sandwiches. They are presented with an FA banner, and the FA gets a red football signed by all the Russian players.

■ **Lord Lang** (81), former Archbishop of Canterbury, dies.

■ Mr William Phelps (87), the world authority on traffic control, the author of the first **traffic** plans for London, Paris and New York, and the originator of the one-way street and roundabouts, dies in Norwalk, Connecticut, USA.

6 Thursday
Mohammedan New Year 1365

The Ministry of Works orders 34 silver-framed **pictures of Hitler** withdrawn from the sale of German embassy goods and chattels.

■ After 12 weeks of negotiation, the agreement is signed on a **US loan** to Britain of £1,100 million. The loan will be repaid over 50 years at 2 1/2% interest, with no repayments in the first 5 years, or in any year when Britain is deemed to have an adverse balance of foreign trade.

■ In a white paper published today, it is revealed that the **gold and dollar reserves** of Britain and the sterling countries in 1941 had fallen to £3 million.

7 Friday

The Morgans cannot find a house anywhere just yet, so the family of three are living in a 12ft x 6ft hut that was a homemade caravan, nr Chippenham, Wilts. It is in two parts— a tiny kitchen and a living room 8 ft x 6ft with a small table and a pull-out bed.

■ A firm of grocers in Manchester has been fined £4,500 for manufacturing and selling **jelly powder** without a licence.

8 Saturday

Hundreds of skilled men are ripping up the floorboards, roads and drains, and cleaning every nook and cranny of the Bridgend Royal Ordinance Factory, and the Welsh Woolwich Arsenal. For the past 6 years these factories have produced high explosives, so any speck of dust might be gunpowder, and a spark from a hammer or a chisel could set off an explosion.

Documents produced at the Nuremberg trials reveal that the Nazis expected **General Franco** to sieze Gibraltar and close the Straits to the Royal Navy in 1940.
■ **Jean Sibelius**, the Finnish composer best known for *Finlandia* and the *Valse Triste* celebrates his 80th birthday.

9 Sunday

Peter, the Scottish **collie** who was a hero of the London blitz, has been demobbed and has retired to Woeley Castle, Birmingham. From his collar hangs the Dicken medal for gallantry. He saved many lives working with the Chelsea rescue squads, once sniffing and burrowing in debris for 10 hours non-stop to find buried people. His finest hour was leading the Civil Defence Parade in Hyde Park, when the King shook his paw.
■ **General George Patton**, commander of the US 15th Army, is **injured** in a car crash near Mannheim, and taken to a hospital in Heidelberg suffering from serious spinal injuries.

10 Monday

General **Eisenhower** has been proposed as the **Republican nominee** for the US presidency in 1948.
■ Only 23,000 of the 60,000 **Poles** in the Polish forces in Britain want to return to Poland.
■ Herbert Morrison, *left,* opens the new Waterloo Bridge, *below,* though Thames fog made it impossible to see from one end to the other.
■ **Princess Elizabeth** (19) sees *Sigh No More* at the Piccadilly Theatre, escorted by two men who had been decorated with the MC by the King earlier that day—Captain Roderick McLeod MC of the Cameron Highlanders, and Mr Charles Villiers MC,ex-Grenadier Guards. After the show the princess went to the Bagatelle Restaurant in Mayfair, where she danced a rumba and a tango.
■ Argentinian dictator Juan **Peron marries** actress **Eva Duarte**; they had already been married in a civil ceremony on October 18.
■ 3ins of snow between Perth and Braemar. London gets its first **snowfall** of winter.

11 Tuesday

William (Lord Haw Haw) Joyce's appeal goes before the House of Lords.
■ US General George **Patton**, injured in a car crash in Berlin on Saturday night, is reported to be **paralyzed** from the neck down.
■ ICI are to build what has been described as the biggest single industrial unit so far in Britain on Wilton Castle Estate, between Middlesbrough and Redcar, North Yorks, one of the beauty spots of the North. Over 3,000 people will be employed.

■ J Arthur Rank's *Caesar and Cleopatra*, the most ambitious and costly film ever made, is top of the box office in London. Based on the play by **George Bernard Shaw**, it was shown to him privately last week. He prefers not to comment on it.

The Best Christmas present of all

12 Wednesday

By December 31, 2,270,000 workers will have made the change from war to peace production. In future, men and women will be able to choose their own jobs unless they are in one of the main industries, i.e. mining, and of call-up age.

■ The Aga Khan's stallion, **Stardust** (a son of *Hyperion*) has been sold to a British syndicate of 40 for £112,000. He went to stud in 1940, and has already made his mark with 8 winners of 15 races last season.

■ The Oxford v Cambridge rugby match is watched by the King, the Queen, and for the first time, Princess Elizabeth. Cambridge wins 11-8.

13 Thursday

Nature lovers, ramblers and cyclists are fighting to save the **Manifold Valley**, Staffs, from being turned into a reservoir by Leicester Corporation.

■ Herbert Morrison says that the State of Emergency will end on February 24 next year, when the Emergency Powers Defence Act 1939 expires.

■ **Norway** has bought £1 million-worth of Spitfires and Mosquitoes.

■ Britain is to bid for the **1948 Olympics**.

... Sold out before publication, the first edition (250,000 copies) of the ABC of Cookery, published by the Ministry of Food...

14 Friday

The King's Birthday

The vicar of St Andrew's,

Broadhurst, Kent, urges his parishoners to bring a hot-water bottle or rug to church to fight the cold.

■ British film star **Patricia Roc**, *below*, is leaving Hollywood to come back to England. She said she had hoped to work with one of Hollywood's handsomest heroes, but nobody paid any attention to her.

■ From April next year the **minimum weekly wages** in New Zealand will be £5.5s a week for men; £2 unemployed; £2 OAPs. Women will get £3.3s.

■ General **Patton**, injured in a car crash last Saturday, is said to be **out of danger**, though he may remain paralyzed for the rest of his life.

15 Saturday

The Ministry of Food asks poultry retailers to halve turkeys this Christmas as there will not be enough to go round.

■ A paraffin lamp and two candles are lighting the office of Mr J B Chiffley, the Australian premier, at Parliament House, Canberra, following the strike of 500,000 workers in New South Wales.

16 Sunday

The Big Three (USA, Russia and Britain) conference opens in Moscow.

■ Lincolnshire sugar industry workers are giving up their Christmas holiday to save the crop from frost. Sugar refining will continue until the New Year, and on Christmas Day alone about 500 tons of refined sugar will be produced.

■ Thousands throng London's East End street markets to do their Christmas shopping. **Petticoat Lane** is virtually at a standstill. Jewellery salesmen have wristwatches for £6 and alarm clocks for 30s. on offer.

17 Monday

The inhabitants of Llanfairpwll-gwyngyllgogerychwyrmdrobwllllantysiliogogogoch, which has only 17 times as many inhabitants as letters in its name, think the name is too long for everyday conversation, and want to change it to Llanfairpg, which a retired schoolmaster (80), says means nothing, or Llanfairpwll, which, he says means less. He suggests that sensible people should call it Llanfairpwllgwyngyll, which means:The 'Church of St Mary in the hollow of white hazel.'

18 Tuesday

From December 31, anybody will be

able to set up in the **retail** trade without a licence.

■ **Randolph Churchill** is sued for divorce by his wife, formerly the Hon Pamela B. Digby.

■ The Nature Reserves Investigation Committee suggest that the following should be preserved as nature schools for student scientists—the **Broads,** the Suffolk coast, Ingleborough, the north and south Downs, the Chilterns, the New Forest, the Lizard, and Dungeness, with national parks in the Lake District, Snowdonia and the Peak District.

■ William (Lord Haw Haw) Joyce's appeal is turned down.

■ The US Army Airforce gives **Orville Wright** a roar past at Kittyhawke, North Carolina, USA.

19 Wednesday

The US Army Air Force are tuning up their **Lockheed** P80s to try to beat the 606mph record of the Gloster Meteor.

■ **War pensions** are to rise, including a 5s a week rise in disablement allowances.

■ **General Patton** (see December 14) is better and is sitting up.

20 Thursday

The Rt Hon **Leo Amery**'s 11th-hour bid to save his son John from execution this morning fails.

■ The government anticipates that the last of five million **demob suits** will be finished by the end of March, and manufacturers will be able to concentrate on producing for civilians and the export trade.

■ The AA is asking private motorists to 'Give a lift to a serviceman or servicewoman' this Christmas.

21 Friday

When the Rev Kenneth Grant of Glasgow, named by the Pope as the new **Bishop of Argyll and the**

Isles, was a PoW in Germany, he asked the Swedish Red Cross for a church. He has received a prefab one, by parcel post.

■ To speed up the **house-building** programme. Mr Bevan frees local authorities to get labour and materials for house building without having to ask Whitehall,

■ **Hollywood** is suffering such a massive **'flu epidemic** that the filming of love scenes has been stopped in most film studios.

■ **General Patton** (see December 19) **dies** in Heidelberg. He will be buried at Hamm US Military Cemetery, four miles from Luxembourg.

22 Saturday

There have been a record number of **divorces** this year—3,000 up on last year, and 5,000 up on 1943.

■ A living crest is being adopted by a town as a victory memorial. Oaks are to be planted on an open space shaped like a shield—the town is **Sevenoaks**, Kent.

■ **Rita Hayworth** divorces **Orson Welles**.

23 Sunday

The 12 year-old son of **Bruno Richard Hauptmann**, executed in 1936 for kidnapping and murdering the Lindbergh baby, has been left £75,000 by an 85 year-old women in New Jersey, who felt that he would be handicapped all his life and wanted to help him.

■ Shepherds armed with **shotguns** are keeping watch over their flocks, as 4,000 sheep have been stolen from the moors of Lancashire and Yorkshire in the last six months.

24 Monday
Christmas Eve

France has forbidden the use of electricity in shops and hairdressers before 10am and after 5pm, and for all advertising outside cafes.

■ **Pandit Jawarhalal Nehru**, former president of the Indian National Congress, tells students in Calcutta that the British

Empire in India has ceased to be, though it may drag on a miserable existence for a little longer.

■ British United Press reports that **Greta Garbo** has turned down an offer to film the life of Georges Sand, the friend of Chopin, the pianist.

25 Tuesday
Christmas Day

The **Guards' Chapel** in Birdcage Walk, London, which was severely damaged by a flying bomb, is open for services again today.

26 Wednesday
Boxing Day

500 Jewish men, women and children, without permits, land on a northern **Palestine** coast. A motorboat manned by armed men of the Hagannah (the Jewish Defence Force) runs a shuttle service to a cargo ship believed to have come from Greece. RAF Spitfires and naval corvettes in the area do not interfere. Non-intervention will be the policy until the Anglo-American fact-finding mission sits and presents its findings.

■ Death of **Admiral Lord Keyes** (73), the man responsible for training the first commandos, and hero of the Zeebrugge Raid and the Dover Patrol.

■ The French **Franc** is **devalued** from £1 = 200 to £1 = 480 (or I franc = 1/2d).

FACES OF THE YEAR

Top row (from left): President Roosevelt, King Peter of Yugoslavia, Winston Churchill, Clement Attlee, President Truman, Princess Elizabeth, William Joyce, Denis Compton.

Centre: Gen. Montgomery, pre-fab homes, Gen. MacArthur, Ann Todd, Queen Elizabeth and King George VI, Josef Stalin, President Tito.

Bottom: Laurence Olivier, Pandit Nehru, Gen. Alexander, King Leopold of Belgium, Ernest Bevin, British servicemen and women.

27 Thursday

Squads of police with dogs track the 500 **illegal refugees** who landed in Palestine yesterday. The Voice of Israel (the Hagannah radio) says they are all safe.

■ A **mistletoe** sprig weighing 50lbs, growing on a lime tree, was cut on a farm at Keynsham, Bristol, during Christmas.

■ The **Duchess of Windsor** is fifth in the list of the world's 10 best-dressed women.

■ Demonstrators in Syria demand the immediate withdrawal of French and British troops.

■ The **International Monetary Fund** is set up with its headquarters in Washington.

28 Friday

For the second year running, **James Mason** is the most popular British film star followed by **Stewart Granger**, *right*, Margaret Lockwood, John Mills, Phyllis Calvert, Rex Harrison, Laurence Olivier, Anna Neagle, George Formby and Eric Portman. Favourite American stars are Bing Crosby, Van Johnson, Greer Garson, Betty Grable, Spencer Tracey, Humphrey Bogart, Gary Cooper, Bob Hope, Judy Garland, Margaret O'Brien and Roy Rogers.

■ £250,000, in British and American **gold coins found** in the German embassy in Spain, is flown to Frankfurt from Madrid in a troop carrier, to be handed to the Allied Control Commission.

■ The Big Three say the **A-bomb** and its secrets will become an international trust, which will have methods of security control to prevent its use by any individual nation.

29 Saturday

Food minister, Sir Ben Smith, sails to the USA today to try and procure more food for 1946.

■ Footballer **Stanley Matthews** has been asked to send a New Year message to Soviet footballers. Their impact on British football has been considerable. The Stoke City manager ws so impressed by the Dynamos playing style that he has decided to adopt it, and Matthews will get a roving commission.

30 Sunday

Freezing fog covers London, the Home Counties, the Midlands and the east coast. In central London bus conductors walk alongside the buses to find the way. Trains from the north reach London four hours late.

■ **Gliding** and sailplane clubs, whose activities were suspended during the war, may begin flying again on January 1.

31 Monday

A **civic reception** is being given to the first boatload of **bananas** to arrive since1940. About eight million of them arrived at Avonmouth yesterday, and the Lord Mayor of Bristol gives a civic welcome to the boat this morning, before the dockers begin to unload the 94,000 stems. The bananas will be stored for a week to ripen, and then they will go to Birmingham, S Wales and SW England for children and young persons under the age of 18, and will cost 1s.1d.lb.

■ Police are searching for two **stowaways** who swam ashore from the banana ship— they were two of the West Indians discovered after the ship had left Jamaica.

■ Dense fog blacks out London, part of the home counties, the Midlands and Lincolnshire. Visibility is down to 10 yards.